Distorted

The Psychology of Gaslighting, the Power of Story, and the Practice of Clarity

Jim Detjen

katapult

Fair-Use & Attribution Statement

Freedom is the freedom to say that two plus two make four. If that is granted, all else follows.

— Georgе Orwell, *1984*

*To those who still trust their own eyes, ears, and instincts —
even when the world insists they shouldn't.*

CONTENTS

PART VI

RESISTANCE

HOW TO LIVE CLEARLY IN A DISTORTED WORLD

Preface

ONCE YOU SEE THE GASLIGHT, YOU CAN'T UNSEE IT. AND ONCE YOU NAME IT, IT BEGINS TO LOSE POWER.

This book is not a manual. It is a lens.

Its purpose is not to hand you instructions but to reveal what you already suspect: reality is being bent as you live it.

Gaslighting isn't theory—it's architecture, woven through headlines, classrooms, boardrooms, even the quiet corners of home. You already breathe the fog. The only question is whether you'll notice it… and whether you'll know how to step outside.

What follows is not a checklist. It is a series of doors. Each chapter opens into an arena—politics, culture, media, technology, even your own mind—where truth is twisted until doubt feels safer than certainty. Repetition, denial, reframing, erosion of trust… these are the fingerprints of gaslighting.

You will not leave these pages with rules. You will leave with sharper instincts.

So consider this an invitation, not an instruction. Step inside. Pay attention. And above all: trust what you see, even when you're told not to.

Part I
The Pattern
What gaslighting is—
and why we fall for it

*The oldest trick in power is not lying.
It's making you doubt you ever knew the truth.*

Gaslighting doesn't start with shouting.

It starts with erosion—one memory, one headline,
one quiet correction at a time.

The first rule is simple:
make you question what you saw.

Not argue.
Not persuade.

Just press until you hesitate.

History proves how easy it is to dim the lights.

Atrocities recast as misunderstandings.
Failures rewritten as triumphs.
Lies archived as fact.

And it never needs your agreement—only your pause.
2

> *Once you start wondering if you imagined it,*
> *the work is already done.*

1

THE ORIGINAL TRICK

HOW DISTORTION BECAME THE
MOST DURABLE FORM OF POWER

A camera pans across a burning street.

The headline says: *"Mostly Peaceful."*

You scroll.

A mother cries on the curb.

A reporter keeps talking.

The chyron stays.

Next clip.

A man loses his job.

The memo calls it *"rightsizing."*

Next clip.

A promise on the campaign trail.

Later: *"What I meant was —"*

Nothing about the facts changed.

Only the frame.

And when the frame shifts fast enough,

memory starts to bend.

Gaslighting doesn't always shout.

It edits.

It smooths.

It reassures.

It speaks in calm voices and confident fonts.

It says, *"Don't overreact."*

It says, *"You're remembering it wrong."*

It says, *"That's not what this means."*

The lights don't go out all at once.

They dim.

One press release at a time.

One correction at a time.

One hesitation at a time.

The oldest trick in power isn't lying.

It's making you doubt you ever knew the truth.

Not chaos.

Choreography.

———

Gaslighting doesn't start with rage.

It starts with revision.

The first cut isn't to truth—

it's to memory.

Psychologists later found that memory bends easier than we think.

In the 1970s, Elizabeth Loftus showed that a single word could change what people remembered seeing.

Ask how fast cars were going when they *contacted,*

and witnesses guessed lower speeds.

Say *smashed,* and they swore they'd seen broken glass that wasn't there.

The brain edits to match the frame.

Language rewrites memory in real time.

That's the danger—

not that you'll forget,

but that you'll doubt.

Memory isn't a vault.

It's clay.

And gaslighters are sculptors.

The Origins of the Term

The word comes from the 1938 stage play *Gas Light,* later adapted into the 1944 film *Gaslight.*

The story is chilling.

A husband manipulates his wife into believing she's going insane.

He secretly dims the gas-powered lights in their home, then insists nothing has changed.

Every protest—"The lights are dimmer!"—is met with denial.

She begins to question her own perception of reality.

She wonders if she's losing her grip.

She becomes dependent on him to interpret the world for her.

It isn't just manipulation—it's the erasure of self-trust.

Case Study · The Lost Photos

In the Soviet Union, propaganda officials didn't just rewrite headlines —they rewrote photographs.

Political opponents were airbrushed out.

Whole families erased from official albums.

The logic was the same as the husband dimming the lights in *Gaslight*: if you can't trust your senses, you must trust the storyteller.

Everyday Gaslights

Think about the last time you told someone you were upset, only to hear,

"You're overreacting."

"You misunderstood."

"You must be remembering wrong."

Sometimes those statements are harmless; humans do misremember.

But the danger lies in repetition.

Hear those lines often enough and you begin to doubt by default.

You stop trusting your memory.

You second-guess your instincts.

Gaslighting at Home

You remember reading the text—clear as day.

The words stick in your head, word for word.

Later, when you check again, it's gone.

Your friend insists they never sent it.

You're left questioning whether the message was real—or if you imagined it.

That's gaslighting in miniature—an ordinary moment that unsettles your trust in memory.

Once that trust wavers, the door is open for bigger doubts, bigger erasures, bigger lies.

Gaslighting at the Doctor's Office

You describe the fatigue, the dizziness, the nights you can't sleep.

The doctor frowns and says, "It's probably stress. Don't worry about it."

You walk out unsure whether you're sick—or silly.

Each moment is small.

String them together, and the haze deepens.

The Scale of Distortion

Individually, these gaslights might seem minor.

But scale them up—practiced by corporations, media outlets, or governments—and they become architecture.

Suddenly we're not debating a misremembered conversation.

We're debating whether the economy is stable, whether a war is necessary, whether freedom still exists.

Gaslighting becomes an institutional weapon.

Practiced on a mass scale, it doesn't just manipulate individuals—it reshapes society.

Historic Parallels

History is full of examples.

- In the United States, the Tuskegee syphilis experiments denied treatment to Black men for decades. When suspicions arose, officials denied wrongdoing until victims questioned their own suffering.
- In Nazi Germany, Jews were stripped of rights, then portrayed as threats. Neighbors saw people rounded up yet were told it was for safety, for order, for the greater good.
- In Baghdad (2003), Iraqis watched bombs fall while Western TV anchors called them "surgical strikes."

Hospitals called them casualties.

The contradiction wasn't just semantic—it was strategic.

Gaslighting isn't a footnote.

It's a recurring chapter in human history.

Case Study · Weapons of Mass Destruction

In 2003, U.S. officials insisted Iraq possessed stockpiles of weapons of mass destruction.

"We know where they are," leaders claimed.

Media outlets echoed the certainty.

When inspectors found nothing, the narrative shifted—the absence itself became proof of concealment.

Grainy satellite images labeled *possible facilities* looked convincing.

Evidence already existed; years later, official reports admitted there were no weapons.

By then, trust had already fractured.

This wasn't just bad intelligence.

It was gaslighting at geopolitical scale—redefining absence as presence, silence as evidence, doubt as disloyalty.

Counter-Moves · Daily Life

Gaslighting thrives in silence and passivity.

Counter-moves are citizen tactics—ways to push back when institutions lean on distortion.

They shift the ground from private confusion to public accountability.

Each move isn't about winning an argument.

It's about preserving evidence, memory, and sanity when the fog presses in.

- **Write down small truths**—conversations, impressions, details.
- **Share your version aloud**—silence is easy to overwrite.
- **Build circles of accountability**—community restores memory.

Gaslighting doesn't need villains.

It only needs repetition.

Repetition is the trick—the constant drumbeat of *you're wrong, you're crazy, you're imagining things.*

It works the same whether it's one manipulative partner or an entire media ecosystem.

The Psychology of Fog

Gaslighting works because it preys on human defaults:

1. **Cognitive laziness**—our brains prefer shortcuts. A confident alternative is easier to accept than to resist.
2. **Need for belonging**—Solomon Asch showed people will knowingly give wrong answers to fit in.
3. **Authority bias**—Stanley Milgram's participants delivered what they thought were lethal shocks because authority insisted.

If the light flickers long enough, we squint until blur feels like stability.

Case Study · Euphemisms in the Modern Era

Consider the Federal Reserve's 2021 description of inflation as "transitory."

Households saw grocery bills and gas prices rise.

Officials insisted the pain was temporary—even healthy.

By the time "transitory" was retired, the damage was done.

Euphemism doesn't hide harm.

It teaches you to rename it.

Every generation invents its own softeners—"rightsizing," "collateral damage," "transitory."

Each one polishes the bruise until you forget what hit you.

The gaslighter takes your glasses and offers to describe what you're looking at.

At first it feels helpful.

Then necessary.

Then you forget you ever had eyes.

———

We live in the loudest information age in human history.

Billions online.

Endless news.

Infinite feeds.

You can watch an event unfold in real time—

and still be told, seconds later,

that you mis-saw it.

It's the perfect climate for mass gaslighting.

Institutions call inflation *healthy*.

They wave off scandals as *conspiracy*—

right up until the evidence cracks through.

Different headlines.

Same instruction:

Ignore what you saw.

Ignore what you heard.

Ignore what you know.

And the moment you comply,

you hand over your sanity.

2

Doubt, by Design

The choreography behind every confident denial

An employee sits down with HR and explains her manager promised her a promotion.

The HR rep flips through the file and replies, "There's no record of that."

She remembers the exact words, the handshake, the late-night email.

But the file is blank. Promise erased.

Gaslighting doesn't begin with shouting.

It begins with something quieter—the confident denial of what you know you heard.

———

The Playbook at a Glance

Gaslighting isn't random.

It follows a script.

Once you see it, you'll spot it everywhere.

- **Deny Reality**—The flat contradiction. "That never happened."
- **Seed Doubt**—The subtle nudge. "Are you sure? Maybe you misremembered."
- **Create Dependence**—The offer of rescue. "I'll explain what really happened."
- **Cement Control**—The closing threat. "Don't bring this up again."

This sequence shows up in marriages, workplaces, media, and politics.

It can feel improvisational in the moment, but step back and the pattern is visible.

Clinicians have long noted how denial and suggestion can destabilize perception.

History has a file on this behavior, too.

The 1938 play *Gas Light* gave the pattern a name—and a mirror.

The Four Steps in Action

1. Deny Reality

The first move is severance: sever your lived experience from the 'official' record.

- **Personal**—"I never raised my voice." (You recorded it.)
- **Corporate**—"Our emissions meet every standard." (They were fined last quarter.)
- **Public**—"No, that crowd photo is doctored." (When it isn't.)

Denial isn't meant to convince.

It's meant to disorient—and if you argue on their terms, you're already playing defense.

> **Counter-move:** Name it out loud: "That's a denial of an observed fact."
> Anchor to evidence—emails, timestamps, receipts.

2. Seed Doubt

Humans are generous with uncertainty; gaslighters weaponize it.

- **Triangulation**—"Everyone else remembers it my way."
- **Memory Jiu-Jitsu**—"You're confusing tone with facts."
- **Tone Policing**—"If you weren't so emotional, you'd see I'm right."

Doubt reframes accuracy as attitude.

You start apologizing for being "confused" when you were actually correct.

> **Counter-move:** Switch to evidence language: "Let's check the record."
> Use a two-column log (Event | Evidence). Writing cuts through the fog.

Resistance in the Small

Take a high-school debate team.

One student misquotes a source in round one: "The Supreme Court ruled this in 1985."

Another student calmly pulls the case-law printout from her binder and reads the actual language.

The fog lifts instantly. The misquote doesn't stick.

Or consider a neighborhood association where a board member insists, "We already voted on that."

A homeowner opens their phone, scrolls to the meeting minutes, and reads the record aloud.

The conversation resets.

These aren't just petty fact-checks.

They're survival drills in miniature.

Each one shows that doubt, once seeded, doesn't have to take root.

The antidote is evidence—calmly presented, in real time.

At work, a project manager announces in front of the team, "We agreed the deadline was Friday."

You remember Monday.

The calendar invite says Monday.

A few colleagues frown but stay quiet.

At home, the same move plays out differently.

A parent says, "You never told me about the recital."

The child remembers handing over the flyer. It's still on the fridge.

Yet the authority in the room insists memory is wrong.

These moments don't look dramatic.

Nobody shouts.

Nobody storms out.

But both scenarios plant the same seed: the suggestion that your recall can't be trusted.

Step Three begins when the "helpful" voice offers to reinterpret reality for you—if only you'll lean on them instead of your own memory.

3. CREATE DEPENDENCE

Once you're unmoored, the gaslighter offers a life raft: "I'll interpret reality for you."

Interpretation replaces observation.

You outsource perception—and grow dependent.

- **In relationships**—"I'll tell you what you meant."
- **In politics**—"Only our network has the truth."
- **In science-by-slogan**—"The debate is over."
- **In workplaces**—"If you check with me first, you won't get confused again."

> **Counter-move:** Diversify inputs.
> One primary source, one opposing analysis, one neutral referee (data, statute, raw footage).
> No single gatekeeper.
> Then practice small assertions: "I saw X. I felt Y." No negotiation.

4. CEMENT CONTROL

Assertions replace arguments.

Questions become disloyalty.

Definitions shift mid-conversation—the moving goalpost.

You're stuck proving yesterday's standard while they play by today's.

Yesterday's "peaceful" becomes today's "violent"—by the same source.

The terms moved; the footage didn't.

> **Counter-move:** Freeze the frame.
> "Let's agree on terms and evidence before we continue."
> If terms keep shifting, end the exchange: "No shared standard, no useful conversation."

Even Volkswagen's "clean diesel"— later exposed as fraud—was sold as innovation.

It shows how denial, doubt, dependence, and control aren't random tricks.

They're a sequence—staged, rehearsed, and repeated.

The Toolkit of Manipulation

Note: *Disagreement or even broad consensus isn't gaslighting.*

The tell is the pattern—shifting terms, selective evidence, and pressure to outsource your perception.

- **Euphemism**—"Rightsizing," "collateral damage," "creative accounting."
- **Contradictory assertions**—Say A and not-A, then accuse you of cherry-picking if you notice.
- **Flood-the-zone**—Drown you in irrelevance until the claim drifts away.
- **Vague appeals to authority**—"Everyone knows…" "Experts agree…" (Which ones?)
- **Whataboutism**—Change the subject while pretending to address it.

  Counter-questions: Which policy? What date? What source? What would change your mind?
  If answers never specify, you're not in a truth-seeking conversation.

Why We Fall For It

- **Belonging and cognitive load**—Tired minds accept loud stories and familiar tribes.
- **Normalcy bias**—We downplay anomalies to keep the world coherent.
- **Sunk cost**—The longer we've believed, the harder it is to switch.

Naming the pressures doesn't make you weak; it makes you prepared.

A sensational headline goes viral on Monday.

By Thursday, a small "clarification" appears behind a paywall.

The original claim lives on in millions of feeds; the correction reaches a fraction.

The lie gets the headline.

Don't share a headline you wouldn't amplify a correction for.

Most people stop looking down long before they notice what's missing.

> **Counter-move:** Save first reports with timestamps.
> Revisit a week later.
> Track deltas between headline and correction.
> Share the update as loudly as the original.

———

Field Guide · Tell-Tale Phrases

Gaslighting often hides in plain sight:

- **"Out of context."** → "Show the full context."
- **"Debunked."** → "By whom? Cite it."
- **"Everyone agrees."** → "Name three independent sources."

When you hear any of these, slow down and switch to evidence mode.

- **Reality log**—Date, time, claim, evidence, outcome. (Paper beats memory.)
- **Witness triangle**—One colleague, one document, one recording (where lawful).
- **Red-team yourself**—Ask, "What would prove me wrong?" Find it.
- **Exit rule**—If terms won't stabilize, disengage. You can't win chess if the pieces keep changing names.

Denial clears the stage;
poetic truth supplies the script.

This is the choreography.

Name the steps; stop the dance.

One receipt, calmly shown, can clear a room.

3
POETIC TRUTH
WHEN STORIES FEEL RIGHT
—AND OUTSHINE THE FACTS

P oetic truth isn't a lie in the ordinary sense.

It's not *"the evidence never existed."*

It's *"the evidence wasn't the point—this meant something more."*

It's how people say,

"We didn't lose—we learned."

Or,

"The numbers mislead, but the spirit was true."

That's poetic truth:

pain rewritten as purpose,

failure reframed as growth,

setback retold as destiny.

And sometimes, that's healthy.

We survive hardship by giving it meaning.

We endure loss by telling a story that lets us move forward.

Poetic truth can heal what data can only describe.

But poetic truth has a shadow.

It can also overwrite facts,

inflate feelings into certainties,

and turn comfort into a substitute for evidence.

That's why Shelby Steele—Pulitzer Prize–winning author and Senior Fellow at Stanford's Hoover Institution—describes poetic truth as a truth that *feels* so morally right it no longer *needs* proof.

His framing captures something essential about our era: narratives no longer compete on accuracy, but on emotional authority.

Poetic truth is:

- **Not a data claim**—but a narrative frame.
- **Compression**—complexity folded into a single moral.
- **Persuasion**—meaning, identity, coherence in one swallow.

———

Useful—even beautiful—

until it stops guiding evidence

and starts replacing it.

Parables work this way.

The Prodigal Son wasn't a case study;

it was a teaching story—its truth wasn't data, it was mercy.

Science speaks in metaphor, too:

gravity as a *force,*

evolution as a *tree.*

The point isn't to banish metaphor.

It's to stay honest about it.

Use the map—just don't mistake it for the territory.

And when better maps arrive, update.

Meaning is magnetic.

It pulls harder than evidence.

Poetic truth doesn't erase facts—

it *outshines* them.

Poetic truth isn't about evidence;

it's about resonance.

It persuades not because it proves,

but because it feels inevitable—sometimes even righteous.

Once accepted, it reshapes perception

in ways facts alone cannot.

Consider how climate debates unfold:

one side presents rising temperatures as a call to save the planet;

another frames the same data as economic sabotage.

The facts are shared; the frames diverge.

A politician doesn't need you to believe every line of a speech.

They only need you to *feel* the story is right—

and the data will come limping after.

COUNTER-MOVES · SPOTTING POETIC TRUTH

- **Ask**—Does this story add meaning—or replace evidence?

- **Separate**—Which part is fact, and which is interpretation?
- **Track resonance**—If it feels "right," pause before assuming it's true.

Why Stories Beat Spreadsheets

Psychologists have long shown why our brains are suckers for story.

1. **Cognitive Ease**—Smooth narratives feel true; messy facts feel suspect. A rhyme, a proverb, a slogan slides past our defenses simply because it takes less energy to process.
2. **Coherence Bias**—We prefer a tidy wrong story over a messy right one. A world that makes sense feels safer than a world that merely reflects reality.
3. **Identity Fit**—When a story flatters our tribe, our guard drops. When it mirrors our group's worldview, we accept it before we ever bother to check it.

Classic lines that illustrate poetic truth's stickiness:

- **"History repeats itself."** (Not exactly—patterns rhyme; specifics differ.)
- **"The market always recovers."** (Eventually? Which market? For whom?)

Case Study · Advertising's Forever Gem

In 1947, De Beers coined the slogan *"A diamond is forever."*

On its face, that's false—diamonds can shatter, be lost, or be sold.

But the line compressed geology, romance, and permanence into one cultural myth.

Within a decade, most American engagement rings carried diamonds.

The poetic truth—*love is proven in permanence, permanence is proven in diamonds*—rewired behavior across generations.

Advertising thrives on poetic truth because data doesn't move markets the way stories do.

No one buys a car because the torque curve is smooth; they buy it because it's *built Ford tough* or because it will *let you find new roads.*

The product might be fine.

The story makes it myth.

CASE STUDY · POLITICS AND THE SLOGAN

In 1917, World War I was sold to the American public as *"the war to end all wars."*

Few slogans better demonstrate poetic truth.

It was tidy, noble, resonant—who wouldn't want to fight one last war to finish them all?

The reality: far from ending war, it set the stage for the most destructive conflict in human history two decades later.

But the phrase stuck because it was emotionally irresistible.

Fast-forward a century: *"Make America Great Again." "Yes We Can."*

Both compress vast political visions into simple, memorable phrases.

They're not policy statements—they're identity statements.

You don't just vote for a candidate; you join a story about who you are.

Poetic truth works in politics because policy is complex but identity is simple.

And when people chant the story, they stop auditing the facts.

CASE STUDY · HISTORY AND MYTH

George Washington and the cherry tree.

You've probably heard it: young Washington, confronted with the fallen tree, confessed, "I cannot tell a lie."

It never happened—fabricated decades later by a biographer.

But it endured because it carried a moral: honesty defines leadership.

The poetic truth outlived the factual one.

Or consider *manifest destiny*, the 19th-century idea that Americans were destined to expand westward.

It wasn't data—it was narrative.

A continent was carved, wars were fought, treaties broken—all under the halo of inevitability.

Poetic truth can build nations.

It can also excuse conquest.

Sometimes we even prefer it that way.

The story feels better than the statistics—so we let it win.

Case Study · Camelot and the American Presidency

After John F. Kennedy's assassination in 1963, his widow Jacqueline told a reporter his time in office should be remembered as *"Camelot"*—a golden age of youth, promise, and nobility.

The story stuck.

Camelot compressed complexity into a single, romantic frame.

It turned a short, turbulent presidency into a legend of lost potential.

———

When Poetic Truth Turns Toxic

Poetic truth isn't always benign.

It curdles when it demands obedience or blocks correction.

The lyric becomes a velvet gaslight—soft outside, coercive underneath.

Patterns of toxic poetic truth include:

- **Feelings as Evidence**—"If it hurt me, it's harmful for everyone."
- Personal pain becomes universal law.
- **Anecdote as Policy**—One story stands in for all, used to justify sweeping change.
- **Teleology**—Outcomes framed as inevitable: "It was meant to be."
- **Halo/Devil Effects**—One trait defines the whole; a single kindness redeems, a single flaw condemns.

Policies often ride on stories that feel right.

Poetic truth can inspire reform—or ossify into dogma when the story outlives the evidence.

THE TAG TEAM · GASLIGHT + POETIC TRUTH

Here's how the two work together:

- **Destabilize**—The gaslighter wipes the slate: "That didn't happen."
- **Soothe with Story**—Poetic truth rushes in: "But we are a resilient people. Onward!"

The lie erases the past.

The poem sells the future.

You're soothed by the story—and less likely to check the receipts.

This tag team appears everywhere:

- **In politics**—A scandal is denied, then reframed as a noble sacrifice.
- **In media**—A correction is buried, but the narrative persists because it feels right.
- **In personal life**—A betrayal minimized, then retold as *"what brought us closer."*

The Survivor's Story

"But he's such a good guy."

That line protects a persona while it erases harm.

Poetic truth—the story we've told about someone—can make factual truth—what they did—hard to hear.

That's when poetry becomes a weapon: charm as cover, narrative as shield.

Why We Believe the Beautiful Lie

The psychological levers are simple but powerful:

- **Illusory Truth Effect**—Repetition makes statements feel true, even when false. One catchy slogan, repeated enough, becomes "common sense."
- **Cognitive Laziness**—It's easier to nod at a proverb than parse messy evidence.
- **Need for Coherence**—A story with a moral feels better than data with caveats.
- **Authority Bias**—When leaders package their agendas as narratives, they ride the halo of poetic truth.
- **Social Proof**—If the crowd cheers the line, dissent feels lonely.

———

Field Guide · Six Red Flags

Want to spot poetic truth in the wild? Look for these signs:

1. **Unfalsifiable morals**—"Good people do X."
2. **Moral licensing**—Virtue is used to excuse harm.
3. **Totalizing labels**—One act defines the whole person or group.
4. **The single vivid case**—One story drives broad policy.
5. **Semantic creep**—Definitions quietly expand to capture opponents.

6. **Applause proofs**—The cheer becomes the evidence.

Poetic truth belongs in your toolbox, not on your throne.

Use story to generate hypotheses—not to declare conclusions.

- **Check**—Ask: What evidence would disconfirm this story? (Name it.)
- **Compare**—What competing story also explains these facts?
- **Calibrate**—What's the smallest claim we can make that still holds?

Facts whisper.

Feelings sing.

Wisdom is learning to hear both—

and to verify the chorus.

The point isn't to banish poetic truth.

It's to keep it in its lane.

Once poetic truth becomes habit, it scales easily.

The same instincts that make us believe personal myths become the raw material for institutional ones.

PART II
THE SYSTEMS

HOW INSTITUTIONS
INDUSTRIALIZED CONFUSION

Power doesn't need truth.
It needs compliance.

Gaslighting doesn't stop at the kitchen table.
It scales.
It systematizes.
It metastasizes.

Here we enter the machinery where stories rule nations—
politics, media, and the bureaucracies that decide what counts as real.

In these systems, distortion isn't a tactic.
It's infrastructure—
the operating system beneath modern power.

4

The Money Script

Economies built on performance, not proof

A cart stops at eggs, then backs away like touching a stove.
The shopper compares last week's receipt to today's.

Overhead, the news declares, "Inflation is cooling."

The paper in their hand says otherwise.

The statement isn't fact—
it's ritual.

Institutions still speak like priests—words that bless without changing anything.

This is the machinery of manipulation.

Unlike the one-on-one gaslight or the individual's poetic truth, institutions run at scale.

They create official stories—backed by resources and repetition—until the story itself becomes the environment.

The statement isn't built to clarify.

It's built to calm.

And the moment calm replaces clarity, you've already started the trade.

And nowhere is that faith language more visible than in the economy itself.

Economics runs on faith disguised as math. Markets rise not on certainty, but on shared belief. That belief is the story—and every story has its priesthood.

————

THE OPERATING SYSTEM OF INSTITUTIONS

- **Bureaucracy as buffer**—The more steps between truth and public, the easier it is to dilute.
- **Euphemism as armor**—*Enhanced interrogation* instead of torture. *Surgical strike* instead of bomb. *Process issue* instead of failure.
- **Repetition as reality**—A phrase echoed often enough becomes "common sense," evidence optional.

Institutions don't need belief.

They just need compliance.

Smooth isn't neutral. It's lubricant. And the bigger the institution, the smoother the spin.

MONEY IS MATH. ECONOMICS IS STORY.

When story drifts from the fridge, you're not mistaken—

you're being asked to ignore your kitchen.

Stories spend easier than numbers.

You don't need a calculator to believe—just a phrase that feels right.

Inflation as "Healthy"

That disconnect becomes doctrine when officials rename pain as progress.

Officials sometimes sell rising prices as a sign of growth.

True in narrow cases—but hollow when wages stagnate and essentials stretch families thin.

The Semantics of Calm

When turbulence hits the economy, the first response isn't policy—it's performance.

Officials step up, delivering reassurance in basis-point increments.

Markets fall; statements rise.

The script is familiar—*"soft landing," "transitory," "temporary correction."*

Each phrase is a sedative, not a statistic.

Language becomes fiscal policy.

Calm is manufactured so panic can be monetized.

If people believe the storm is *"contained,"* they keep spending.

Press releases start to sound pastoral.

Volatility becomes *"normalization."*

Recession becomes *"technical adjustment."*

When words sand down pain, accountability slips with the dust.

The story doesn't fix the wound—it numbs it.

But the new priesthood doesn't hold press conferences—it writes algorithms.

The Invisible Hand, Coded

The market once ran on rumor; now it runs on code.

Algorithms trade in microseconds, chasing headlines they help create.

Artificial intelligence no longer waits for consensus—it predicts, prices, and moves on.

Prices shift automatically, reacting to signals few can see.

A keyword in an earnings call moves billions.

A sarcasm misread by a sentiment model shaves points off a stock.

This is the new abstraction of power—

systems that cannot explain themselves but insist they're objective.

The invisible hand now hides inside a black box.

Its logic is opaque, its tone polite, its reach total.

When error looks like precision, trust slides from evidence to output.

Faith used to rest in markets, then in experts. Now it worships code.

The National Debt

U.S. debt is projected to exceed $37 trillion by 2026, according to Congressional Budget Office and Treasury forecasts.

Abstract—until it hits pensions, interest rates, or foreign leverage.

The story told: *"Debt is just numbers on a ledger."*

The unspoken risk: when faith in repayment falters, numbers become consequences.

CASE STUDY · THE 2008 CRASH

The refrain was, *"No one saw it coming."*

Not true.

Economists, journalists, even homebuyers spotted the bubble inflating.

Those who warned were dismissed as alarmists.

The myth of endless growth drowned out the flashing red data.

Independent researchers broke the spell.

Then the story collapsed.

CASE STUDY · BAILOUTS AND "TOO BIG TO FAIL"

When massive firms collapse, taxpayers foot the bill.

The spin: *"We're protecting the system."*

The reality: profits are privatized; losses are socialized.

Translation: the public pays.

CASE STUDY · THE BUYBACK BOOM

For decades, stock buybacks were marketed as confidence—companies "returning value to shareholders."

But the modern buyback boom tells a different story: extraction dressed as optimism.

Instead of funding research or wages, corporations spend trillions buying their own shares.

Earnings-per-share rises, stock prices climb, executives cash out.

On paper, prosperity. In practice, stagnation.

In 2023, U.S. firms repurchased nearly $950 billion of stock—the largest sum on record.

Worker productivity flattened. Real wages barely moved.

It wasn't growth. It was choreography.

The distortion works because the chart points up.

We mistake rising lines for rising lives.

> *The miracle of modern capitalism*
> *isn't creation —*
> *it's recycled applause.*

Case Study · Enron's "Innovation"

In the late 1990s, Enron was celebrated as a corporate pioneer.

Magazines called it *"America's most innovative company"* six years in a row.

Behind the curtain, the "innovation" was fraud—off-book entities hiding billions in debt.

The myth of vision smothered the math.

When collapse came, pensions evaporated and trust cracked.

Lesson: Institutions don't just mislabel failure—they mythologize it until the myth collapses under its own weight.

Shrinkage and Shadows

Inflation doesn't always announce itself.

Sometimes it hides in the package.

Twelve ounces becomes ten.

Restaurant tips migrate from gratitude to mandate.

Airlines unbundle seats from oxygen.

Everything costs slightly more, delivers slightly less.

Official statistics say inflation is "cooling."

Your grocery bill disagrees.

The difference hides in metrics that ignore substitution and shrinkage.

Shadow inflation thrives between what's measured and what's felt.

When officials cite "stable prices," they mean the basket, not the burden.

Each small reduction teaches compliance.

We adapt, downgrade, adjust.

It isn't deceit in one product—it's erosion in a thousand small bites.

The economy doesn't need to lie;

it just needs you tired enough to stop noticing.

Everyday Gaslights in Economics

- "The market always goes up." (Not in every sector, not for every generation.)
- "Unemployment is low." (If you don't count those who stopped looking.)
- "Housing is affordable." (Based on national averages that ignore local collapse.)

Counter-Moves · Spotting Spin

- **Translate euphemisms** into plain speech.
- **Archive contradictions** for later comparison.
- **Ask:** *Who benefits if I believe this?*

If money runs on story, so does memory.

And stories of the past are hardest to balance.

> *When systems protect distortion,*
> *people pay the bill.*

5

The Memory Hack

Who owns the past when it's editable?

F ront page.

"Mayor Implicated in Corruption Probe."

Weeks later, after the details unravel, the correction is buried in a column on page 17.

The narrative sticks.

Guilty or not, the mayor becomes a punchline.

Media doesn't just report events.

It magnifies some facts and minimizes others.

Distortion didn't start with cameras; it began the moment history learned to edit itself.

———

Case Study · Columbus "Discovered" America

For centuries, textbooks declared that Columbus "discovered" America—a phrase half-truth, half-anthem.

It captured the wonder of exploration, but not the world that existed before he arrived.

The first chapters of our national story weren't malicious; they were selective.

A new republic reached for symbols that could bind it together, even if it meant trimming what didn't fit the page.

But selection becomes distortion when it hardens into certainty.

History is never finished; it's rewritten every time a culture decides what to remember.

> *The test of a mature nation*
> *isn't whether it edits—*
> *it's whether it edits honestly.*

Case Study · "Mostly Peaceful Protests"

Television screens in 2020 showed burning cars, shattered glass, boarded windows.

The chyron beneath read "Mostly Peaceful Protests."

That juxtaposition wasn't an accident.

It was framing.

If enough people accept the phrase, the fire behind the reporter becomes noise instead of signal.

Balance demands noting the opposite tactic too.

In 2003, a massive "Mission Accomplished" banner framed the Iraq War as victory.

Reality was years of grinding insurgency.

Both phrases—"Mostly Peaceful" and "Mission Accomplished"—show how institutions frame memory before history is written.

CASE STUDY · THE BIOGRAPHY AS BATTLEFIELD

Once, history meant centuries.

Now it means your name in a search bar.

A public figure clicks their own Wikipedia page and finds a version of themselves they've never met—assembled from hit pieces, hostile columns, and selective omissions.

Neutral formatting. Loaded framing.

Bethany Mandel called her entry "a curated collection of my worst moments."

Philip Roth tried to correct his own page; editors rejected him—he wasn't a "reliable source" on himself.

The reflection stood; the reality didn't.

A biography becomes a battleground disguised as an encyclopedia.

The fight isn't over facts—it's over framing.

CASE STUDY · THE REWRITE

History doesn't vanish all at once. It gets edited.

A new textbook arrives: fewer pages on slavery, more on "economic migration."

Another edition shortens the Vietnam War to two paragraphs.

Each change small enough to pass unnoticed; together they shift the moral gravity of a nation.

Wikipedia mirrors the same churn.

Pages expand, shrink, reframe overnight.

An event still happened, but now it "lacked context."

An atrocity becomes a "conflict."

Facts remain—meaning changes.

The rewrite never admits itself—it calls the update progress.

And progress is easy to defend when only the previous version knows what was lost.

The Algorithm that Edits History

Libraries once deleted by neglect; now deletion is design.

Search engines decide what appears first—and what drifts into oblivion.

Links expire. Headlines update. Old versions vanish from the public cache.

Each tweak feels technical, not ideological.

But code has bias.

A story tagged "controversial" sinks; a partnered outlet rises.

A search for a crisis returns brand content about "resilience."

Digital memory isn't neutral shelving—it's an auction.

The result is softer than censorship, harder to trace.

No books are burned; they're simply unindexed.

Forgetfulness becomes a feature of design.

In a world without deletion,
the algorithm invents forgetting.

———

The Funhouse Archive

Transparency was supposed to save the project.

Every edit logged, every discussion public.

Yet sunlight doesn't disinfect when the mold lives in the code.

WikiScanner once traced anonymous edits to government and corporate IP addresses—including the halls of Langley.

Today, the fingerprints are subtler: coordinated editors, moderation bots, sentiment algorithms.

Each tweak tiny enough to escape notice; together, they tilt the record.

Recent analyses suggest roughly five percent of new entries now involve AI assistance, which means the machine is learning its bias from the same pages it helps polish.

Distortion teaching distortion—an infinite regress of confidence.

No trench coats, no secret files.

Just a glowing cursor rewriting the footnotes of history.

When the edit button becomes the eraser, transparency turns to theater.

You can watch the change happen—you just can't stop it.

And once the record itself becomes entertainment, attention replaces accuracy.

The Meme that Replaced Memory

Every age condenses itself into images.

Ours chooses memes.

A photo from a protest replaces the protest itself.

A five-second clip defines a year.

Complexity can't compete with catchiness.

Virality turns nuance into slogan, tragedy into template.

The deeper the wound, the faster it trends—until repetition sterilizes shock.

Tomorrow's historians will cite screenshots as primary sources.

They'll measure public feeling by retweet counts.

The record will survive, but the context will not.

THE COMFORT OF FORGETTING

Erasure doesn't always arrive from above.

Sometimes we help it.

Forgetting simplifies loyalty.

Doubt is exhausting; clarity is lonely.

Believing the simpler story keeps dinner conversations intact.

Memory is work.

Forgetting is rest.

And rest, offered by authority, feels merciful.

> *The first luxury of every empire*
> *is amnesia.*

Institutions study this mercy and turn it into curriculum.

EDUCATION AS CURATED MEMORY

A student can quote modern slogans but can't name the century of the Constitution.

Ask who fought the Civil War, and many hesitate.

Ask when America was founded, and answers scatter by decades.

Education doesn't just transmit knowledge.

> *It edits memory —*
> *sometimes by subtraction.*

History once followed a timeline—discovery, founding, trial, reform.

Now it drifts through themes: power, identity, grievance.

The sequence is lost; the continuity breaks.

Textbooks linger on recent movements yet rush past the ideas that built the country—limited government, federalism, the Bill of Rights.

Students learn about protest before they learn what the Constitution protects.

That's the quieter crisis.

Not revision, but erosion.

A generation fluent in criticism but illiterate in context.

When history becomes only a list of mistakes, patriotism sounds naïve.

When it becomes only a string of triumphs, it turns to propaganda.

Somewhere between pride and shame lives truth—and we're forgetting how to find it.

Schools don't need to make citizens feel good or bad about the past.

They need to make them *capable* of recognizing it.

Civic literacy isn't nostalgia; it's maintenance.

A republic that forgets its story eventually forgets itself.

An education that loses memory
doesn't liberate a nation—
it untethers it.

Institutional Motives

Why does the machinery run this way?

- **Self-preservation**—Admitting fault risks collapse. Story buys time.
- **Efficiency**—It's easier to sell "peacekeeping" than admit occupation, or "discovery" than admit conquest.
- **Power**—A unified narrative keeps people aligned. Confusion keeps them compliant.

Within that power hides another rule—the *perennial source*.

Legacy outlets define reliability; dissenting ones are tagged "unreliable," their citations erased.

The archive doesn't argue; it excludes.

Truth becomes a membership privilege.

Take wartime briefings.

The official story is almost always "progress."

The reality may be stalemate—or retreat.

Leaders bet that morale matters more than accuracy.

The story becomes policy.

Gaslighting confuses the person.

Poetic truth persuades the crowd.

Institutions scale both—until society forgets who lit the first lamp.

Language doesn't just describe power.

It is power.

When words shift beneath your feet,

memory becomes the only solid ground left.

The fight over memory always ends in headlines—because whoever edits the story edits the past.

The next edit isn't in the archive—it's on the homepage.

6

THE MEDIA MIRROR

WHEN HEADLINES DICTATE MEMORY

You scroll your feed.

A video auto-plays: fire in the background, a chyron that reads "Mostly Peaceful."

Another swipe: a celebrity apology, polished by PR until it means nothing.

Distortion doesn't rest; it refreshes with every swipe.

Comments split instantly—half declare it truth, half call it propaganda.

Welcome to media in the age of emotional truth:

facts framed by feeling, clarity blurred by hashtags, reality compressed to fit a screen.

———

THE FIRST FRAME WINS

Cognitive science calls it the primacy effect—first information weighs heaviest.

Media gaslighting isn't always deceit.

Sometimes it's the speed premium—being first, not accurate.

Corrections rarely undo impressions.

The update whispers.

The chyron shouts.

> *If the first story is wrong,*
> *the truth arrives too late.*

And by the time it catches up, people have already built arguments, friendships, and grudges around the wrong version.

Nobody likes rebuilding on fresh ground.

When Headlines Tell Half the Story

Headlines aren't meant to inform; they're meant to hook.

Research from Columbia University and Inria found approx. 59 percent of links shared on social media were never clicked (2016).

Writers know this.

So the gaslight can live entirely in the title.

- "Violence Erupts" vs. "Police Respond."
- "Record Profits" vs. "Consumer Prices Soar."
- "Experts Say" vs. "Some Experts Warn."

Each phrase scripts emotion before facts arrive.

A protest turns tense.

Cameras find the one burning car, not the thousand calm marchers.

"Riots Erupt" trends; *"Protest Concludes Peacefully"* never will.

Both are technically true.

Both distort by scale and focus.

Gaslighting hides not in the fact itself,

but in the chosen frame.

The Crisis Carousel

News cycles run on adrenaline:

- Storm coverage with reporters standing in puddles.
- "Market Crash" headlines triggered by a half-percent dip.
- Election "upsets" called before polls close.

The carousel spins you between panic and relief.

The crash may be small, but the fear is massive.

Dizzy people rarely notice the ride operator—and that's the point.

Spin the audience fast enough and they'll thank the carnival for the ride instead of asking where their wallet went.

The Vanishing Correction

Buried on page A17: *"An earlier version misstated…"*

Online: a footnote—*"Updated for accuracy."*

By then, the original claim had already gone viral.

The damage isn't misinformation; it's erosion—of attention, of proportion, of trust.

Corrections whisper where headlines screamed.

> *The lie gets the billboard.*
> *The truth gets the broom.*

Speed spreads confusion faster than fact.

What disappears next isn't data—it's confidence that truth can still be found.

When truth gets an umpire, the crowd stops checking the rulebook.

We built a new priesthood of truth—the fact-checkers, the platforms, the "independent verifiers."

Their intent began noble: slow the spread of lies.

But once the referees step on the field, they become part of the game.

Every correction carries a frame, and every frame carries bias.

The illusion of neutrality becomes its own gaslight: *Trust us—we're impartial.*

A post appears online. Within seconds, a gray box wraps it: " 'Independent fact-checkers have determined this claim to be false.' "

Relief floods in. No need to verify; someone else already has.

That's the quiet comfort of the modern referee.

They promise safety from confusion—but deliver dependence.

Once, fact-checkers aimed to serve the reader.

Now they serve the algorithm's incentives.

Labels decide what travels and what disappears.

"Misinformation" becomes a moving target—defined not by evidence, but by consensus.

Referees begin as guardians, then become gatekeepers.

Censorship no longer burns books; it quietly de-ranks them.

Visibility becomes permission.

Silence becomes verdict.

Authority bias does the rest.

A statement wrapped in expert consensus feels true even when it isn't.

The badge replaces evidence; tone replaces test.

Gaslighting evolves not by calling truth false,
but by training you to stop checking.

When truth gets an umpire, the game stops being about evidence.

It becomes about authority.

The whistle signals not accuracy, but obedience.

Evidence is mixed.

And that's the point.

The danger isn't that algorithms radicalize everyone—

it's that they monetize outrage faster than reason can catch up.

We measure clicks because conviction takes longer.

SIDEBAR · THE FACT-CHECKER'S FRAME

Fact-checkers claim to clarify the fog—but often create their own.

- A politician's claim stamped *False*, but the rating hinges on an obscure metric.
- A viral story marked *Missing Context*, but the added context tilts the frame more than it resolves it.
- Some claims checked instantly; others vanish unexamined.

These aren't corrections. They're calibrations—reality tuned to the preferred frequency of the day.

When interpretation masquerades as resolution, the message becomes:

Don't trust your eyes.
Trust ours.

The danger isn't the lie.

It's the stamp that says the debate is over.

Manufactured Outrage

Outrage sells better than calm.

Networks crop clips for heat, not light.

Algorithms reward whatever spikes pulse rate—anger, shock, fear.

The result isn't clarity.

It's monetized cortisol.

Your feed rewards what you hate.

Anger clicks harder than reason.

Media gaslighting rarely invents facts.

It just emphasizes feeling until evidence fades.

- A celebrity trial becomes about how she looked on the stand, not testimony.
- A policy debate scored by optics instead of outcomes.
- A tweet with 100 likes outruns the correction with 100 views.

Emotional truth spreads faster because it feels right.

And once enough people feel the same thing, *correction* feels like betrayal.

Case Study · The Video Edit

A politician pauses mid-sentence:

"We will… not tolerate corruption."

The clip cuts after *"We will."*

Shared widely, it becomes proof of corruption.

By the time the full video surfaces, outrage is already fossilized.

Hashtags as Narrative Weapons

Hashtags compress complexity into chant.

They're not neutral; they're framing devices.

- **#BelieveAllWomen**—moral appeal that skips due process.
- **#DefundThePolice**—one phrase, dozens of meanings.
- **#StayHomeSaveLives**—public health turned pressure slogan.
- **#TreatYourself**—self-care as marketing loop.
- **#GoodVibesOnly**—positivity as silence.
- **#StopTheSteal**—a legal process recast as loyalty test.
- **#BackTheBlue**—solidarity reframed as obedience.

The power—and the danger—is portability.

Hashtags travel faster than facts and harden faster than evidence.

Counter-Moves · The Ferguson Frame

In 2014, the shooting of Michael Brown in Ferguson, Missouri, became a national flashpoint.

Early headlines repeated the claim that Brown had his hands up when he was shot—"Hands up, don't shoot."

The phrase spread overnight: a chant, a hashtag, a moral shorthand.

Months later, federal investigations documented conflicting witness accounts and inconclusive forensics.

The Department of Justice confirmed systemic racial bias in Ferguson policing—

and reported that "Hands up, don't shoot" was not supported by the Brown case evidence (2015).

By then, the narrative had hardened into cultural truth—

repeated as evidence rather than examined as claim.

The danger wasn't protest.

It was narrative inflation: a slogan becoming the whole truth while the facts were still being sorted.

Psychologist Stephan Lewandowsky calls it the continued-influence effect:

even after correction, first impressions keep shaping belief.

We remember emotion, not evidence.

Everyday Cultural Gaslights

You don't need breaking news to feel the fog.

It shows up everywhere:

- AI art marketed as "authentic creativity."
- Health apps rebranding 800 calories of ice cream as "cheat-day balance."

None of these are outright lies.

Each just chips away at the line between reality and performance.

Memes flatten complexity into instant certainty.

A photo plus seven words can outweigh a 5,000-word essay.

Memes don't argue; they ridicule.

And ridicule is harder to refute than rhetoric.

- **Read past the headline**—Truth hides in paragraph nine.
- **Compare outlets**—Overlap reveals what's real.
- **Pause before sharing**—Time exposes exaggeration faster than fact-checkers.
- **Notice emotion**—If it spikes anger or relief, it's probably framing you.
- **Save first drafts**—Screenshots, clippings, scribbled notes outlast the algorithm's amnesia.

Your memory is your archive.
Guard it.

If you don't, someone else will edit it—

and sell it back to you as news.

Headlines frame the story.

Language frames the headline.

The next distortion doesn't come from cameras or chyrons,

but from the words themselves—

how they soften, swap, and blur until the sentence feels kind while the meaning disappears.

That's where we go next.

7

THE WAR ON WORDS

EUPHEMISM, SPIN, AND THE DISAPPEARANCE OF PLAIN SPEECH

A warplane drops a bomb.

The report calls it a *surgical* strike.

The language doesn't soften the blast—it sanctifies it.

A company fires three thousand people.

The memo calls it *rightsizing.*

A government raises taxes.

The press release says *revenue enhancement.*

Language doesn't just report violence.
It edits empathy before conscience can protest.

Nothing about the facts changed—only the words.

But the words changed the response.

That's linguistic gaslighting—language that edits emotion before it reaches conscience.

———

The Euphemism Economy

Euphemisms are compromise: soft words for hard truths, sold in bulk.

Sometimes that's mercy: *passed away* gives grief room to breathe.

But when institutions weaponize softness, euphemism becomes erasure.

- *Collateral damage* turns civilian deaths into spreadsheet errors.
- *Friendly fire* makes killing your own troops sound like a barbecue mishap.
- Ethnic cleansing sanitizes genocide.

The language doesn't lie outright.

It removes the sting long enough for policy to proceed.

Ancient Rome practiced *damnatio memoriae*—chiseling disgraced names off stone.

Modern institutions don't chisel.

They rebrand.

Vietnam taught *pacification* (burning villages) and *incursion* (invasion).

The Gulf War added *servicing the target* (killing people) and *degrading assets* (blowing things up).

Each phrase buys distance you'd never grant face-to-face.

> *The smaller the word,*
> *the bigger the denial.*

Orwell named it in 1946: political language makes lies sound truthful and murder respectable.

The wind only got more sophisticated.

When a word turns toxic, swap it.

- **Torture**—*enhanced interrogation*
- **Firing**—*rightsizing, restructuring, workforce adjustment*
- **Propaganda**—*public diplomacy, strategic communications*

Before 9/11, waterboarding had a history—prosecuted as torture since World War II.

Rename it and you move the debate from *Should we torture?* to *What counts as torture?*—a bureaucratic hallway instead of a moral door.

The Senate's 2014 report listed the techniques: simulated drowning, 180-hour sleep deprivation, coffin-sized boxes, stress positions, threats against families.

Brutal. Unreliable. Misrepresented.

Senator John McCain said it plainly:

"It is torture."

The euphemism still survived in memos.

And outside government memos, corporations discovered the same anesthetic power of tone.

THE PLATFORM OF CARE

Corporations once hid behind profit.

Now they hide behind compassion.

Tech companies announce *trust and safety* initiatives that quietly throttle speech.

Censorship becomes *content moderation for well-being.*

Data harvesting becomes *personalization for connection.*

Every policy arrives wrapped in empathy.

When language feels kind, resistance feels cruel.

Users agree to new terms not because they understand them but because they sound humane.

HR once said *diversity and inclusion.*

Platforms now promise *belonging and safety.*

The vocabulary of care expands faster than the boundaries of freedom.

The softer the tone, the sharper the knife beneath it.

Outside the boardroom, the same leverage belongs to labels.

Political Language

Labels tilt perception; the label becomes the argument.

Win the wording, tilt the mind.

- *Death tax* vs. *estate tax*—same policy, different reflex.
- *Illegal alien* emphasizes criminality; *undocumented* emphasizes paperwork.
- *Global warming* alarms; *climate change* sounds like weather.

No side is neutral.

Frames are tools.

Whichever frame dominates shapes the facts people are willing to hear.

Counter-Moves · The Language of War

A missile lands.

The report calls it a *precision strike.*

Civilians die.

The phrase survives.

Governments rarely say *kill.* They say:

- neutralize targets
- eliminate threats
- surgical operations

Language recasts destruction as hygiene.

"Collateral damage" launders grief through grammar.

"Smart munitions" promise morality by circuitry.

Each word distances the hand from the harm.

Warfighters see reality up close.

It's the briefers who reframe it.

The gaslight belongs to those writing the talking points, not those on the ground.

War doesn't erase violence; it redefines it until mercy sounds mechanical.

Criticizing the narrative of war isn't rejecting those who fight it.

It's refusing to let their courage be edited by press releases.

Weaponized Labels

Some words no longer describe behavior—they assign guilt.

Racist. Nazi. Fascist.

Once reserved for genuine evil, they now function as conversational grenades—thrown whenever persuasion fails.

Some words don't persuade—they punish.

Denier. Extremist. Phobic.

Each one ends the argument before it begins.

The inflation is moral, not grammatical.

When every disagreement is "hate," real hate hides in the crowd.

When every opponent is a "fascist," the word stops warning and starts flattering the accuser.

Language meant to expose tyranny now licenses it.

The accusation becomes a reflex, the meaning dissolves, and serious words lose the power to shock.

The louder the label, the hollower the meaning.

DEHUMANIZING LANGUAGE

"Dehumanizing" once meant stripping people of dignity to justify harm.

Now it's invoked whenever someone feels uncomfortable.

That inflation isn't compassion—it's confusion.

Real dehumanization isn't hearing a hard truth.

It's when power convinces you that someone's humanity is conditional.

When labels replace faces and disagreement becomes evil, gaslighting completes its work.

That's not sensitivity.

It's soft tyranny disguised as empathy.

CORPORATE DOUBLESPEAK

The same grammar that shields states now shelters companies.

A short glossary:

- *Synergy* = we merged and cut heads
- *Aggressive accounting* = fraud
- *Streamlining* = cutting corners
- *Flexible scheduling* = unpredictable hours, no control
- *Right-to-work* = restricted union power

A memo says, "We're eliminating jobs to increase efficiency."

Translation: layoffs.

Efficiency sounds virtuous by design.

Jobs sound abstract—until they're mortgages.

If a policy sounds like progress but feels like extraction, translate it.

Counter-Moves · The Green Lexicon

Every era invents words to bless its appetites.

Ours chose *sustainability*.

"Clean diesel."

"Beyond Petroleum."

"Carbon-neutral."

Each one a prayer for progress that leaves the math untouched.

Volkswagen sold purity while its engines choked cities.

BP planted a sunflower on its logo while 96 percent of its revenue (approx.) stayed in oil and gas.

The words worked better than the machines.

That's the genius of the green lexicon—language that absolves before it acts.

When morality becomes a marketing department, grammar does the laundering.

The gaslight isn't the pollution.

It's the poetry that hides it.

Academic Fog

Sometimes precision needs jargon.

Sometimes jargon protects weak ideas.

If "problematize hegemonic discourse" is just another way to say "question power,"

then say question power. Clarity doesn't need camouflage.

Feynman's test still holds:

If you can't explain it to an undergraduate, you might not understand it—or you might not want others to.

Every generation invents new jargon to hide its uncertainty.

Yesterday's scholars wrote in Latin; today's write in abbreviations.

The goal is the same—turn understanding into membership.

If comprehension requires a password, you can charge tuition for translation.

When the academy confuses meaning, the newsroom completes the loop.

The Media Spin Cycle

The same reflex that softens policy now softens news.

Editors call border crises *migration surges;* anchors call lies *claims;* fact-checkers call disagreement *disinformation.*

Words change faster than events.

"Crisis" becomes "challenge."

"Failure" becomes "shortfall."

Each substitution cools the temperature by a degree until outrage sounds impolite.

When journalism fears judgment, vocabulary replaces verification.

Language stops revealing; it reassures.

> *Words meant for light*
> *become filters for glare.*

THE LOADED QUESTION

Language doesn't just label.

It directs.

- "When did you become so angry?"
- "Don't you care about the planet?"
- "Why are you so defensive?"

Each question corners rather than clarifies.

Answer once, and you've already agreed to the accusation.

Refuse the premise instead:

- "That assumes I'm angry; I'm not. Here's the specific claim."
- "Caring about the planet is exactly why I disagree with this policy."

Loaded questions aren't inquiry.

They're assertion with a question mark.

———

- **Translate to plain speech**—*rightsizing → layoffs; enhanced interrogation → torture.*
- **Name the frame**—"That question assumes X; I don't accept X."
- **Demand specifics**—"Which metric? Which policy? What changed since last month?"
- **Note drift**—"Last quarter you called it X; now it's Y."
- **Preserve the original**—screenshot, save, compare. The delta is the tell.

Words are territory.

Guard the map or someone else redraws it.

A Memo Lands

A memo lands.

Restructuring appears 17 times.

Layoffs appears zero.

Everyone knows what it means.

That gap—between the polished phrase and the lived reality—

is where the fog lives.

Words shape the argument.

Politics decides who gets to define them.

Every era has its code words.

They begin as tools for order and end as fences for thought.

> *Clarity isn't style—*
> *it's courage.*

———

THE DEATH OF DEFINITION

Every civilization begins by naming things.

Every decline begins when it stops agreeing on what the names mean.

Words like *truth, justice,* and *science* once pointed to shared realities.

Now they point to tribes.

"Follow the science" can mean opposite things depending on who says it.

"Justice" can describe both prosecution and protest.

The more universal a word becomes, the less weight it carries.

When definitions blur, power fills the vacuum.

If nothing is fixed, everything is flexible—and someone always profits from flexibility.

Control the dictionary,
and you control the debate.

THE DICTIONARY AS PARTICIPANT

Once, dictionaries were observers.

Now they are participants.

For centuries, lexicographers recorded usage after culture decided it.

Today, revisions race to catch—or to lead—the next moral shift.

"Preference" becomes "phobia."

"Man" and "woman" stretch until biology bows to ideology.

In 2020, one major dictionary quietly redefined "sexual preference" as offensive the same day a senator used it in a hearing.

The timing wasn't linguistic. It was political.

Definitions now move at the speed of outrage.

Words that once anchored conversation now drift with the current.

Language no longer records change; it performs it.

> *When meaning updates by press release,*
> *truth becomes a subscription service.*

Reclaiming Plain Speech

The cure for distortion isn't counter-jargon.

It's honesty that sounds almost impolite.

Plain language risks offense because it removes the cushion.

But that's also what makes it moral.

When we speak clearly, people can finally disagree clearly.

Clarity doesn't divide us; it defines the terms of peace.

> *Precision is not cruelty.*
> *It's respect.*

When language decides what can be said, politics decides who is allowed to say it.

Words shape belief; politics rents the echo.

8

THE POLITICAL FRAME

HOW LANGUAGE REPLACES ACCOUNTABILITY

E lection night.

The crowd cheers as results trickle in.

Two networks call it early.

Another hedges: *"Too close to call."*

A candidate steps up to the mic: "We won. It's over."

Hours later, precincts keep reporting.

The race isn't over.

The victory speech still circulates.

Supporters remember it as settled fact.

Politics runs on persuasion —
until persuasion hardens into gaslighting.

Not "vote for me because." But "reality already favors me—so you're wrong to question it."

The trick isn't just to win votes.

It's to win the memory of the night—

before the last ballot is counted.

And every generation rewrites election night in its own dialect of certainty.

Across parties, the vocabulary shifts but the tactic stays the same.

From Watergate's *"modified limited hangout"* to today's *"alternative facts,"*

every era tests whether language can outlast evidence.

The Left rebrands legislation for optics—an 'Inflation Reduction' bill that, by subsequent measures, did not reduce inflation.

The Right reframes taxes as relief even when deficits rise.

Both sides rename policy until disagreement feels immoral.

Deny · Reframe · Repeat

Politics loves the three-step loop: deny what happened, reframe what it means, repeat until memory conforms.

- A handshake becomes *"never met."*
- A scandal becomes *"fake news."*
- A recorded vote becomes *"taken out of context."*

By the time evidence resurfaces, repetition has hardened the new "truth."

Authoritarians don't win by one perfect lie;

they win by a firehose of falsehood—volume so high that correction can't keep up and exhaustion replaces judgment.

———

Manufactured Consensus

When officials say *"Everyone agrees"* or *"The science is settled,"*

they're not reporting truth—they're enforcing compliance.

Consider how pandemic policies were framed: dissent wasn't debated; it was pathologized.

Once you're cast as the lone dissenter, silence feels safer than skepticism.

This isn't about majority opinion.

It's about weaponizing the fear of being alone.

The Language of Half-Truths

Political gaslighting thrives on euphemism:

- *Enhanced interrogation* = torture.
- *Kinetic action* = war.
- *Collateral damage* = civilian deaths.
- *Revenue enhancement* = tax hike.

Language recasts harm as order.

The glossary becomes a fog machine.

Outrage feels unreasonable.

Change the word—and you change the response.

That's why politicians obsess over labels.

Call it a *tax* and people revolt.

Call it a *contribution* and people nod along.

Same dollar—different spell.

- **Moving goalposts**—A pledge to *"balance the budget"* becomes *"reduce the deficit"* becomes *"slow spending growth."*
- **Contradictory claims** —A policy is both *"unprecedented"* and *"routine."*
- **Whataboutism**—Any critique answered with *"But what about your side?"*

The goal isn't conviction. It's surrender through exhaustion.

Shrug. Comply. Move on.

In politics, power doesn't follow truth.

It edits it.

And the red pen never runs out of ink.

Case Study · The Shifting Crowd

At a rally, cameras pan a half-empty stadium.

The campaign claims the shots are *"deceptively framed."*

Wide angles surface.

Next claim: *"Thousands were outside and turned away."*

Drone footage circulates.

Next claim: *"The drone footage is fake."*

Each contradiction forces supporters to choose loyalty over evidence.

By the end, allegiance—not footage—defines the crowd size.

What matters isn't who exaggerated first, but how fast we forget the calibration.

The impulse isn't confined to one party.

In 2020, some outlets cropped protest photos to make modest gatherings look massive;

others framed the same scenes as chaos.

Different lenses, same distortion.

The *"alternative facts"* moment wasn't about headcounts.

It was a test: can any side make you doubt photographs?

> *If you can be gaslit about what you see,*
> *you can be gaslit about anything.*

CASE STUDY · WATERGATE AND THE LONG DENIAL

In 1972, five men were arrested for breaking into the Democratic National Committee headquarters at the Watergate complex.

The White House response was simple: deny.

Dismissed at first as a *"third-rate burglary,"* Watergate became a master class in deny–reframe–repeat.

Even as evidence piled up, the administration insisted nothing was proven.

Each denial bought time; each reframing cast critics as partisan.

By Nixon's resignation in 1974, the scandal had already reshaped how Americans saw power—

not that leaders sometimes lie,

but that leaders could engineer reality long enough to survive.

Watergate remains the template:

deny, reframe, repeat until trust itself becomes collateral damage.

THE "THREAT TO DEMOCRACY" NARRATIVE

Few political phrases have spread as quickly or stuck as firmly as *"threat to democracy."*

The gaslight hides in the framing.

A genuine threat—coups, voter suppression, censorship—is serious.

But the phrase now stretches to cover everything from campaign-finance disputes to procedural votes.

Repetition recasts ordinary disagreement as existential.

At the same time, *"threat to democracy"* doubles as poetic truth.

It offers moral clarity, emotional weight, urgency.

Like *"Make America Great Again"* or *"Yes We Can,"* it functions less as description and more as declaration.

Gaslight + poetic truth: destabilize trust in opponents, then reassure your side with a rallying cry.

The fog thickens, and each election feels like the last.

The Psychology of Political Fear

Political gaslighting works because it leans on human defaults:

- **Conformity pressure**—As Asch showed, people will knowingly give wrong answers to avoid standing out.
- **Authority bias**—As Milgram found, obedience trumps conscience when commands wear credentials.
- **Tribal loyalty**—Identity research shows people defend their side even when it contradicts facts—because rejecting the group feels like rejecting themselves.

Political gaslighting isn't about changing facts.

It's about securing belonging.

Once your tribe defines reality, doubting the story feels like betraying yourself.

Everyday Political Gaslights

Not every manipulation makes headlines.

Some slip into stump speeches, press briefings, or debate soundbites—
ordinary phrases that blur reality a little more each time:

- *"Historic legislation."*—Routine bills inflated into mythic victories.
- *"Common-sense reform."*—Casts opponents as irrational by definition.
- *"No evidence."*—Often means "no evidence we're willing to accept."

These phrases aren't lies outright.

They're fog—soft-focus lenses that blur reality until voters stop resisting.

Headlines often sane-wash incoherence—translating a ramble into *"an economic plan."*

It soothes the reader and gaslights the viewer who saw the unedited version.

Misinformation is wrong by accident.

Disinformation is wrong on purpose.

The fix differs: one responds to correction; the other feeds on chaos.

Counter-Moves · Voters

- **Keep a personal archive** of promises and receipts.
- **Compare headlines** against primary sources.
- **Refuse to outsource memory** to institutions.
- **Notice the pivot**—*"What I meant"* is the tell.
- **Vote on pattern, not promise**—performance is the receipt.

The strongest defense against political gaslighting is a personal archive of truth.

Institutions will rewrite the record.

The only question is whether they'll overwrite yours.

And the shovel is our desire to belong.

And once politics perfects the script, culture turns it into instinct.

What leaders rehearse, audiences perform.

9

THE CULTURAL REWRITE

HOW COLLECTIVE BELIEF REPLACES COLLECTIVE MEMORY

P olitics trains perception; culture performs it—the same choreography, different stage.

Remember the blue-and-black dress?

Or was it white-and-gold?

For weeks, the same photo split the Internet in half.

Friends argued at dinner tables.

News anchors ran segments.

Nobody changed their mind.

But suddenly your eyes felt less trustworthy.

Three years later came *Yanny vs. Laurel*—one clip, two entirely different sounds.

The same divide.

The same doubt.

Proof that perception isn't fragile.

It's negotiable.

If our eyes and ears can't agree on a dress or a word,

what chance do we have when politics and media get involved?

Now raise the stakes: a teenager posts a dance video.

Overnight, strangers call it *brave, problematic, empowering,* and *toxic.*

Same clip.

Same steps.

Four entirely different verdicts.

Culture doesn't just set trends.

It scripts how you should feel about them.

And when enough voices echo the same script,

culture becomes a mirror—a beautifully lit illusionist—reflecting not who you are, but who you're expected to be.

Culture as Consensus

Culture thrives on agreement—what we wear, what we celebrate, what we cancel.

But agreement often comes from repetition, not reflection.

- A phrase trends; soon it's everywhere.
- A meme defines a group.
- A single scandal sets a narrative for millions who never saw the act.

This isn't persuasion by evidence.

It's persuasion by belonging.

Loneliness outweighs evidence every time.

Most people would rather be wrong together

than right in isolation.

The Meme Effect

Memes distill complex events into a single image or caption.

They travel faster than facts—and soon, they define the story.

- A politician's lifetime of work reduced to one awkward photo.
- A celebrity's identity reframed by a five-second clip.
- A tragedy trivialized into punchline form before the facts are clear.

A meme doesn't have to lie outright.

Its power lies in shaping what people remember first—

and what they stop questioning later.

Once humor became habit, outrage found its algorithm.

The Outrage Economy

Anger isn't just emotional fuel—it's the new currency.

Platforms discovered that outrage keeps people scrolling longer than joy or empathy.

Every argument, every viral feud, every public apology feeds the same machine.

Outrage feels moral. It functions like marketing. That's the trick— virtue with a business plan.

The more indignant you are, the more valuable your data becomes.

Modern culture doesn't sell products first.

It sells feelings that justify them—belonging, grievance, virtue.

What looks like activism often behaves like advertising—sincerity for rent.

As algorithms later proved, outrage wasn't just emotional—it was profitable.

> *The algorithm doesn't care what side you're on.*
> *It only cares that you stay angry enough to click again.*

That indifference is the design.

Cancel Culture and Selective Memory

Cancellation may start with critique,

but it quickly rewrites history.

Past successes vanish, nuance evaporates,

and entire careers collapse into a single offense.

Reverse gaslight—*They were always terrible.*

History shrinks to a mugshot of the worst moment.

The danger isn't accountability.

It's the denial that people can grow.

When we flatten change into contradiction,

memory becomes punishment.

Cultural Rebranding

History is full of reputations rewritten by cultural gaslighting:

- Artists ignored in their lifetimes become "geniuses" centuries later.
- Yesterday's heroes recast as today's villains.
- Words themselves shift—*tolerance, liberation, authenticity*—until their meanings dissolve.

Culture rewrites the dictionary without telling you it picked up a pen.

By the time you notice the ink,

the definition has already changed.

And you're the one accused of *misusing* the word.

THE CELEBRITY MIRAGE

Celebrities are mirrors for cultural gaslighting.

- **Musicians** shift from *"voice of a generation"* to *"dangerous influence"* without changing a lyric.
- **Athletes** hailed as heroes for victory are vilified for opinion—sometimes within the same broadcast.

The culture that crowns them also scripts their downfall,

then reframes it as hindsight.

CULTURAL CONTRADICTIONS

Culture thrives on mixed signals because contradiction generates attention.

- ***"Be yourself"***—but not like that.
- ***"Speak your truth"***—but only if it trends.
- ***"Celebrate diversity"***—but only the curated kind.

The faster the swing, the harder the balance.

That's the design—and the profit.

The whiplash isn't a bug—it's the feature.

The more the ground shifts, the less likely you are to plant your feet.

Counter-Moves · The Icon Flip

History keeps rewriting its cast to fit the mood of the moment.

Martin Luther King Jr., branded radical in his own day,

is polished into a safe motivational icon.

Britney Spears—once dismissed as a breakdown in progress—

reframed as a victim of exploitation.

Each revision carries truth—

but when the new narrative insists it's the only truth,

cultural gaslighting takes hold.

Counter-Moves · Colin Kaepernick's Knee

In 2016, NFL quarterback Colin Kaepernick knelt during the national anthem to protest police brutality.

Overnight, the act was reframed in clashing narratives:

to some, a courageous stand;

to others, a disrespectful attack on the flag.

Years later, the framing keeps shifting.

Advertisers embrace Kaepernick as icon.

Politicians invoke him as wedge.

The kneel hasn't changed.

The narrative has.

Cultural memory isn't about the act.

It's about the story that wins.

Cultural Gaslighting in Identity

- **Generational labels**—cohorts reduced to stereotype.
- **Fashion policing**—yesterday's "unprofessional" becomes today's "authentic."
- **Moral licensing**—brands claim virtue (*eco-friendly, fair trade*) while outsourcing the opposite.

The Moral Marketplace

Even morality now runs on trend cycles.

Causes rise and fade with the same tempo as fashion drops.

One month, silence is violence.

The next, exhaustion becomes virtue.

Corporations borrow each movement's language, stamp it on merch, and call it solidarity.

Consumers buy redemption at checkout.

*Righteousness has become retail —
priced in attention and worn
until the next season of outrage arrives.*

The Algorithmic Amplifier

Social media doesn't just reflect culture.

It engineers it.

- Algorithms amplify extremes.
- Moderate voices vanish.
- Consensus online isn't real—it's curated.

You're told *"everyone is outraged."*

In reality, it's a handful of loud accounts—

boosted by code that rewards outrage over accuracy.

Even Facebook's internal research confirmed it—divisive content keeps you scrolling.

The anger wasn't organic.

It was optimized.

THE PSYCHOLOGY OF CULTURE

Culture persuades not with proof but with patterns.

- **Social proof**—if millions share it, it feels true.
- **Moral contagion**—outrage travels faster than nuance.
- **Bandwagon effect**—once a side seems to win, neutrality feels like cowardice.

These aren't facts.

They're reflexes.

> *Repetition doesn't prove truth.*
> *It just trains response.*

Consensus isn't discovered.

It's engineered—and sold back to you as belonging.

- Note when language suddenly shifts.
- Track how *normal* gets redefined.
- Compare meanings across generations.
- Pause before sharing outrage that flatters your tribe.

When culture trains what to feel,

schools train what to ask.

Normal isn't discovered.

It's manufactured.

And once manufactured,

it's marketed back to you as if you demanded it.

Institutions may script the story,

but the cost is always paid in people.

The fog outside becomes the pressure inside—

classrooms, courts, and workplaces where belief replaces reason.

This is where distortion stops being abstract

and starts rewriting lives.

And nowhere is that rewriting more deliberate than in the classroom.

Part III
The Human Cost
The fog inside our most human systems

*The fog outside matters
less than the fog inside your head.*

Beyond institutions, gaslighting seeps inward—
reshaping how people think, feel, and even see themselves.

These chapters trace its toll:
on minds,
on justice,
on workplaces,
on families.

If the fog blankets society,
this is where it blinds the self.

10

The Classroom Rewrite

EDUCATION'S QUIET WAR ON CURIOSITY

High-school gymnasium.

Parents gather for curriculum night.

A teacher assures them, "We're simply teaching critical thinking."

Weeks later, homework comes home with scripted *reflection prompts* that steer toward one conclusion.

Students aren't asked to think.

They're asked to echo.

Education at its best sets minds free.

At its worst, it gaslights—telling you the page means the opposite of what you see; that curiosity is suspect, that experts will think for you.

———

THE HIDDEN CURRICULUM

Every school teaches two curriculums:

1. **The official syllabus**—math, science, history.
2. **The hidden one**—values, assumptions, interpretations.

The hidden one is where gaslighting creeps in:

- "This is the only correct reading of history."
- "This theory is no longer debated."
- "If you question this framework, you don't belong here."

The lesson isn't on the board; it's in the questions you learn to swallow.

HISTORY REWRITTEN

Textbooks update regularly—but not always for clarity.

- Atrocities minimized or renamed.
- Achievements reframed through today's lens.
- Figures once celebrated quietly vanish.

Revision is natural.

The danger is when it's sold as continuity—*"It was always taught this way."*

That's textbook gaslighting.

> *Whoever controls the curriculum*
> *controls the future.*

And the scariest part?

Most parents never see the fine print. They trust the brochure because it sounds like care.

In the Soviet Union, textbooks didn't just evolve—they obeyed.

Lessons that once praised a scientist could, overnight, erase him.

History flexed to ideology until memory itself served the state.

Every age rewrites inconvenient lessons.

The difference now is that edits happen digitally,

invisibly,

instantly.

Illusion of Mastery

Universities announced: *"You don't need the SAT or ACT anymore."*

It sounded liberating.

The fog remained.

Applications soared, rankings climbed,

and scholarships still favored those who played the old game.

Two decades earlier, *No Child Left Behind* worked the same trick.

Classrooms narrowed to the test.

Officials praised claimed 'proficiency gains.'

Years later, colleges admitted staggering remediation rates.

That wasn't progress.

Merit isn't flawless.
But erase it, and all that's left
is favoritism dressed as fairness.

That's brutal.

You've weaponized common sense.

———

HIGHER EDUCATION AND IDEOLOGICAL PRESSURE

On college campuses, gaslighting often wears the costume of *inclusivity* or *safety*.

- Controversial speakers disinvited as "dangerous."
- Grading rubrics reward alignment over rigor.
- Departments claim "academic freedom" while policing which questions count.
- Mandatory pledges—loyalty oaths in the McCarthy era, DEI statements today—use the same mechanism: *align or be excluded.*

Different virtue, same reflex.

Some professors were told to issue *trigger warnings* before discussing sensitive material.

The goal sounded compassionate.

Critics noted that warnings often discouraged engagement.

The gaslight wasn't kindness.

It was selling avoidance as resilience.

When protection replaces preparation,

education loses its edge.

When schools protect students from ideas,
they aren't educating.
They're indoctrinating.

Wrap the muzzle in kindness,

and students thank you while their range of thought disappears.

The Debt Narrative

"College is an investment."

That line reframes crushing debt as savvy foresight.

Graduates leave with six-figure loans and thin job prospects.

The response: *"You chose the wrong major."*

The Technology Mirage

Tablets replace textbooks.

Schools tout "21st-century learning."

Scores stay flat.

Tech companies call it progress—even when outcomes stall.

Students become test subjects in billion-dollar experiments

where the story is *innovation* and the reality is distraction.

Counter-Moves · The Vanishing Subject

Across the country, certain subjects shrink quietly—civics, shop, art.

The official line: *"Students need STEM skills for tomorrow's jobs."*

The result: education without context, skill, or soul.

The gaslight: *"You don't need this. We're future-proofing you."*

Education that deletes memory trains compliance, not wisdom.

Compliance looks like success—until real life asks questions the
textbook never did.

Cultural Gaslights in Classrooms

- Wellness weeks that paper over exhaustion with pizza parties.
- Self-esteem inflation—every child "above average."
- Mission statements promising "excellence for all" while quietly triaging resources.

The slogans recast failure as progress.

The Death of Curiosity

The first casualty of gaslighting is wonder.

Learning once began with uncertainty; now it begins with risk assessment.

Before students raise a hand, they measure the cost.

What if the question sounds unfashionable?

What if the example offends?

What if the answer contradicts the rubric—or the teacher's worldview?

Ideology no longer lives only in manifestos.

It seeps into grading rubrics, reading lists, and the tone of "approved" discussion.

Most teachers don't silence curiosity outright—but the system quietly rewards agreement until curiosity feels like defiance.

In many classrooms, curiosity feels dangerous—not because students are timid, but because the boundaries are invisible and constantly shifting.

The lesson arrives early: *safety lives in silence.*

By college, students speak fluently in caution.

They edit their thoughts before anyone else can.

At elite universities, the effect hardens into habit.

Bright minds whisper opinions in hallways they won't voice in seminars.

They trade honesty for belonging, and the trade feels rational.

Inquiry has been replaced by performance.

Students learn to echo consensus, not test it.

The goal is no longer to understand, but to survive the discussion.

When curiosity dies,
education stops being discovery
and becomes reputation policing.

The Psychology of Learning Fog

Education gaslighting taps the brain's defaults:

- **Authority bias**—students assume the teacher's frame is neutral.
- **Survivorship bias**—those who thrive in the system mask those excluded by it.
- **Conformity pressure**—silence buys safety; dissent feels like deviance.

Learning fog doesn't just blur what you know.

It trains you not to notice.

Once you stop noticing, the gaslight doesn't need to argue.

It just hums.

Curriculum by Framing

A parent attends curriculum night.

The teacher promises "critical thinking all year."

The reading list looks fine—no obvious gaps.

Then the slide deck appears: *"Lived experience over primary evidence."*

Debates become reflections.

Claims become feelings.

By November, grades reward agreement more than analysis.

The content never changed.

The frame did.

Counter-Moves · Students and Parents

- Track curriculum changes over time.
- Compare textbooks with primary sources.
- Ask: *What's missing? What's not being asked?*

Receipts Beat Retweets

A tenth-grader quotes a viral explainer in history class.

Another opens the primary packet—dates, margins, evidence.

The room quiets.

The explainer's clean story doesn't match the messy source.

Eyes lift.

Silence, then a nod.

No one yells.

No one scores points.

They simply learn again that records beat retweets.

> *When protection replaces preparation,*
> *the mind locks itself.*

That's how you walk into the fog—without losing yourself.

And when learning turns to performance, justice soon follows the same script.

11

PROCEDURE AS PERFORMANCE

JUSTICE THAT FOLLOWS EVERY RULE—AND STILL FAILS TRUTH

The jury files in.

The verdict is read: "Not guilty."

Gasps ripple through the gallery.

For weeks, the public watched footage, followed testimony, weighed evidence in the court of opinion.

The official line: "Justice was served."

For some, relief.

For others, betrayal.

For everyone, dissonance.

Justice is supposed to be the bedrock of truth.

But when courts, police, or lawmakers twist language, conceal context, or reframe outcomes,

justice itself becomes the stagecraft.

Justice as Theater

Courtrooms run on ritual: robes, gavels, phrases polished by centuries of certainty—performance mistaken for proof.

But when outcomes conflict with common sense, ritual gaslights by insisting:

"Because we followed procedure, the result must be just."

Procedure isn't truth.

Justice can follow every rule and still miss the truth standing in front of it.

Body-cam footage is requested on Monday, *"still processing"* on Wednesday, and *"under review"* on Friday.

By the following week, a spokesperson announces a *"careful investigation"*—just as a clip leaks online.

The official statement pivots: *"Taken out of context."*

A longer cut surfaces.

New pivot: *"Ongoing litigation prevents comment."*

By the time the full video surfaces, the story has already changed outfits.

The leak, not the act, draws the outrage.

No direct lie—just a practiced sequence of delay, reframing, and ritual language

that teaches the public to mistrust their sight.

Historical Parallel · Show Trials

Every regime perfects its own theater; only the costumes change.

In Stalin's Soviet Union, courtrooms became theaters of fear.

"Confessions" were extracted under torture but presented as voluntary testimony.

Verdicts were predetermined, yet each trial carried the solemn rituals of justice—robes, judges, closing arguments.

The gaslight wasn't only for the accused.
It was for the public,
who learned to doubt their own doubts.

If a neighbor confessed on live radio, who were you to question whether it was real?

The form of justice was preserved.

Its content was hollowed out.

The Plea-Bargain Machine

Approximately ninety-five percent (Justice Dept. 2022) of U.S. criminal cases end in plea deals, not trials.

Prosecutors present overwhelming charges, then "offer" reduced time if defendants plead guilty.

Many accept—not because they're guilty, but because the risk of trial is terrifying.

The illusion: *"You admitted guilt."*

Reality: many plead guilty just to survive.

Consider a nineteen-year-old first-time defendant, accused of a felony he insists he didn't commit.

The prosecutor offers: *"Plead guilty to a misdemeanor, six months probation."*

Trial carries ten years.

His public defender whispers, "Take the deal."

He signs.

Later, the conviction bars him from jobs, housing, even loans.

Roughly one in five people later exonerated by DNA had pled guilty first—

survival math disguised as confession.

People spend decades behind bars for crimes they never committed—

while the system insists it was certain.

The distortion isn't just the sentence.

It's the story: *"We were right then,"* and *"We're right now"*—

even when the evidence proves otherwise.

Counter-Moves · The Central Park Five

In 1989, five teenagers in New York City were arrested and charged in the brutal assault of a jogger in Central Park.

Interrogated for hours without lawyers or parents, they eventually signed coerced confessions.

The public was told justice had been swift and certain.

Years later, DNA evidence and a confession from the real perpetrator exonerated them.

By then, each had spent years in prison.

The official story—*"We got the right men."*—collapsed.

The distortion wasn't just the conviction.

It was the years of being told, in courtrooms and headlines alike,

that their own innocence was a lie.

Even exoneration couldn't erase the scars.

Policing Narratives

Headline: *"Suspect Resisted Arrest."*

Later footage: the suspect was sitting handcuffed on the curb.

Early headlines echo official statements.

By the time video surfaces, memory splits:

Do you trust your eyes—or the institution sworn to protect you?

Every scandal prompts the refrain: *"This was an isolated incident."*

Communities living with repeated patterns feel gaslit:

"If it's isolated every time, why does it keep happening at all?"

Justice gaslighting thrives on time lag—

truth delayed long enough for doubt to root.

The Fog of Law

- *"Excessive force"* → *"reasonable action."*
- *"Out of an abundance of caution"* → *"We're limiting transparency."*
- *"Ongoing litigation"* → *"Time is our friend."*
- *"Procedure was followed"* → *"Truth unaddressed."*

We treat verdicts as sacred,

but the rituals of justice can be their own fog.

The robe becomes costume, the gavel a prop, the transcript a script.

What feels like transparency is sometimes theater—

an institution telling the audience to trust the play, not the performance.

Defendants, victims, and communities alike are told

not to trust what they saw, heard, or experienced—

only the legal glossary.

QUALIFIED IMMUNITY

The doctrine sounds neutral—*"clearly established rights."*

In practice it means this:

unless a prior case ruled against the exact same conduct,

in nearly the same way,

there's no remedy.

The absurdity is the point.

Immunity becomes impunity.

———

THE PSYCHOLOGY OF JUSTICE GASLIGHTING

Why do people accept verdicts that clash with common sense?

Psychology offers clues:

- **Authority bias**—Jurors and the public instinctively defer to uniforms and robes.
- **System justification**—We prefer to believe our system is fair; doubting it feels destabilizing.
- **Status-quo bias**—Once a jury rules, acceptance feels safer than outrage.

It doesn't need to erase evidence—

only to cloak it in ritual and authority until the public doubts their own doubts.

The Gaslight of Law

The rule of law is supposed to outlast the passions of the moment.

It anchors power to principle.

But when leaders praise the law in speeches and defy it in practice, the anchor drags.

Governors ignore U.S. Supreme Court orders.

Legislators vow to "resist" rulings they dislike.

Mayors declare they will not enforce federal decisions.

Each insists it's for a higher cause—justice, safety, compassion.

Both sides claim fidelity to law while choosing which laws count as real.

This is gaslighting at the constitutional scale—obedience reframed as oppression, defiance sold as moral courage.

Citizens are told, "We're protecting democracy," even as leaders decide which parts of it to obey.

The poetic truth of law is unity under principle.

The gaslit version is selective enforcement wrapped in virtue.

Once power decides which verdicts are valid,

the rule of law becomes narrative.

And when truth itself becomes partisan,

justice no longer binds—it performs.

The Moral Root of Law

The rule of law rests on something older than statutes.

The founders understood that.

Before government could secure rights, it had to acknowledge they came from somewhere higher than government itself.

The argument that the Declaration's logic grew from Christian belief is still debated.

Some hear Enlightenment echoes of reason and natural law.

Others hear the cadence of Scripture—Creator-endowed rights, equality before God, justice that answers to heaven.

The founders likely heard both.

Either way, the claim was radical: human dignity is not a favor from kings but a fact of creation.

That conviction once tethered law to something immovable.

When we lose that tether, justice drifts with fashion.

Rights become preferences.

Equality becomes rhetoric.

And truth—once anchored in moral realism—starts floating downstream with power.

Gaslighting enters when meaning detaches from source.

Poetic truth takes its place—language that still sounds noble but no longer binds to anything real.

Without an authority above politics, distortion becomes strategy and narrative becomes law.

The words remain, but their definitions migrate with whoever holds the microphone.

When principle stops appealing to the eternal, it starts negotiating with the loudest.

COUNTER-MOVES · HOLDING JUSTICE ACCOUNTABLE

- Time-stamp every request and response—timelines expose choreography.
- Translate legal jargon into plain speech—if nothing remains, ask again.

- Track early statements against final evidence—note what shifted.

Because in the fog of ritual,

the only lamp left may be your own notes.

> *Justice unrecorded*
> *is justice rewritten.*

Procedure without transparency is theater.

And in the workplace, the script doesn't change—it just switches stages.

12

THE VANISHED AGREEMENT

HOW WORKPLACES REWRITE THEIR OWN PROMISES

Monday morning.

Staff meeting.

The slide reads: *"No layoffs this year."*

Applause. Relief.

Two months later, half the department is gone.

The email calls it a *"strategic restructuring."*

In the next all-hands, leadership insists the company is *"stronger than ever."*

Everyone nods anyway.

Silence is safer.

———

THE LANGUAGE OF SPIN

Companies love euphemisms:

- "Right-sizing" instead of layoffs.
- "Streamlining" instead of cutting benefits.
- "Talent mobility" instead of churn.
- "Optimization" instead of layoffs.

Each word reframes loss as progress.

Employees are told not to trust their shrinking paycheck—

but to trust the *vision* on the slides.

If the story shines, the numbers can vanish—

until payday comes, and the shine doesn't cover rent.

Metrics as Mirage

Promises vanish.

Concerns get denied.

Metrics drift: one week the outcome is churn, the next it's touchpoints —whichever flatters the slide.

Percentages balloon: *up 200 percent*—from one to three.

Success is defined by the easiest ruler at hand.

> **Counter-move:** Freeze the frame.
> Write down the metric, the denominator, and the start date.
> When the numbers change, ask: Did the reality improve—or just the math?

Case Study · The Performance Review

An employee is told their *"communication is lacking."*

They ask for examples. None are given.

When they adapt, next year the critique shifts: *"Too aggressive."*

The gaslight: "We're helping you grow."

Reality: the system ensures compliance.

Mission Statements vs. Reality

- A company preaches *"work–life balance"* while praising all-nighters.
- Posters shout *"We are a family."* HR policies prove otherwise.
- "Diversity and inclusion" headlines marketing while pay gaps persist.

The mission isn't what's on the wall.
It's what happens in the hall.

The Burnout Spin

Exhausted teams are told: *"You just need to be more resilient."*

Wellness programs appear—free yoga, mindfulness apps, gratitude challenges.

Workloads stay impossible.

Burnout is recast as personal flaw, not organizational failure.

If exhaustion is weakness, the system never has to change.

It's not the firehose drowning you.

It's your lungs for not keeping up.

Resilience without rest isn't resilience.
It's surrender.

The Moral Myth of Mercy

Institutions discovered what corporations already knew: virtue sells.

Modern wars arrive draped in compassion—humanitarian intervention, stabilization mission, defense of democracy.

Corporate life follows the same script.

The language of care has replaced the language of command.

"People-first leadership." "Holistic wellbeing." "Belonging."

Every policy now wears the tone of tenderness.

When language performs care, questioning it feels ungrateful.

> *The poetic truth is mercy;*
> *the policy is management.*

When morality becomes strategy, dissent feels disloyal and skepticism ungrateful.

Employees aren't asked to comply—they're asked to believe.

Every layoff becomes compassion.

Every demand becomes purpose.

Every exploitation wears the smile of care.

Work becomes worship.

The paycheck is practical; the mission is spiritual.

Together they build the most efficient faith system of the modern age—

one where meaning is manufactured, devotion is measured,

and every sermon ends with a quarterly report.

Gaslighting by Silence

Sometimes denial isn't spoken. It's implied.

Leadership knows about toxic managers, broken systems, looming cuts.

Employees ask questions and hear: "Don't worry. Everything's fine."

Silence buys compliance—until the reveal, when shock replaces trust.

Then come the all-hands calls, the "tough decisions," the applause for "transparency."

Gaslighting isn't always what's said.

Propaganda by Omission

Sometimes the gaslight isn't a lie.

It's a silence.

In boardrooms as in governments, the most effective manipulation is omission.

- Civilian casualties uncounted.
- Jobs erased without notice.
- Harassment reports closed "for confidentiality."
- Ethics breaches buried in audits no one reads.

When the record goes quiet, the narrative writes itself.

It's the same choreography everywhere—whether on a battlefield, a balance sheet, or a press release.

The loudest gaslight is often the one that never speaks.

Gaslighting in HR

Human Resources should protect employees—but often protects the company.

Reports of harassment become *"misunderstandings."*

Patterns of discrimination become *"isolated incidents."*

HR's language persuades employees that harm is normal.

Historical Parallel · Ford's "Five-Dollar Day"

In 1914, Henry Ford stunned industry leaders by doubling wages to five dollars a day.

Headlines called him visionary.

Workers lined up for prosperity—missing the fine print.

Ford's *Sociological Department* inspected homes, habits, even personal lives

to decide who deserved the full wage.

The gaslight: "This is generosity."

Reality: control.

A century later, companies still use perks to mask surveillance and leverage.

Field Guide · Public Spin

Corporate gaslighting has its own phrasebook:

- "A sophisticated attack by state actors" → Our security was sloppy.
- "A regrettable incident" → We're dodging liability.
- "Accounting irregularities" → We got caught.
- "Unplanned downtime" → We weren't prepared.

Public statements gaslight not just employees but the public—

erasing accountability with polish.

Case Study · Enron's Culture of Spin

If Ford's gaslight was paternalism, Enron's was brilliance.

At its peak, Enron was hailed as *"America's most innovative company."*

Employees were told they were building the future of energy.

Inside, profits were booked before they existed; losses hidden off the books.

Staff were told to trust leadership's brilliance even as the math stopped adding up.

Whistleblowers were dismissed as disloyal.

When collapse came in 2001, thousands lost jobs and pensions.

The lesson wasn't just fraud—it was how corporate gaslight convinces insiders to doubt their own spreadsheets

until the edifice collapses.

The Promotion Mirage

Promises of advancement dangle like carrots.

Employees deliver more, work longer, chase the next title.

When promotions never come, leadership reframes: *"You're gaining valuable experience."*

Translation: free labor, no raise.

The Psychology of Workplace Gaslighting

Why do smart employees go along with contradictions they can see?

- **Authority bias**—When a manager says it's fine, people default to agreement.
- **Conformity pressure**—Speaking up risks being labeled "negative."
- **Survivorship bias**—Success stories hide the burnouts and quiet exits.

Gaslighting doesn't erase evidence.

It exploits our instinct to defer, conform, and hope.

- Keep your own records—notes, emails, summaries.
- Separate mission statements from hallway reality.
- Call out euphemisms by translating them to plain speech.

Forget the slogans.

Keep the files.

Memory outlives spin.

In workplaces, memory is leverage.

> *The one who keeps the receipts*
> *keeps the power.*

The same denial that corrodes workplaces eventually seeps into hospitals.

Bureaucracy doesn't heal.

It just rehearses its excuses.

And in medicine, the rationalizations come wrapped in compassion—

soft words that hide hard neglect.

13

WHEN CARE DISTORTS

MEDICINE'S PARADOX: THE SYSTEM THAT GASLIGHTS ITS PATIENTS

Hospital waiting room.

Fluorescent lights hum.

A nurse says, "The doctor will see you shortly."

Ninety minutes later, the doctor enters: "We value your time."

Your experience says otherwise.

———

Medicine is supposed to be anchored in evidence.

Yet patients often find themselves gaslit—told symptoms are *"in your head,"*

side effects are *"rare,"*

and that the system is working even when it plainly isn't.

The authority gap in medicine runs both ways.

Patients hesitate to question doctors; doctors hesitate to question specialists.

Certainty gets rewarded faster than curiosity.

Admit doubt, and you risk looking incompetent—so many don't.

The result isn't always arrogance; sometimes it's fear disguised as confidence.

But either way, the silence sounds the same: *"Trust me."*

When Symptoms are Dismissed

- "It's normal for your age."
- "It's just stress."
- "You're overreacting."

Patients—especially women and minorities—report being told their pain is exaggerated.

Later, diagnoses reveal conditions ignored for years.

The gaslight isn't always malicious.

It's systemic bias reframed as certainty.

When Serena Williams nearly died after giving birth, she warned doctors she was short of breath and needed a scan.

They dismissed her—until tests revealed multiple clots in her lungs.

If one of the world's most recognized athletes has to fight to be believed,

what happens to everyone else?

Ask anyone who's heard, *"All tests are normal,"* while their body screams otherwise.

The Illusion of Clean

Gloves look like hygiene.

Employees slip them on; customers relax.

Then they touch the register, the trash, the fridge—and the food.

In practice, gloves spread more bacteria than clean hands ever would.

This is poetic truth at work: the symbol of safety replacing safety itself.

Authority blesses the illusion, and everyone accepts the story.

Medicine has its own gloves—practices that look safe, feel modern, and sound reassuring,

even when evidence says otherwise.

Historical Parallel · Lobotomies

In the mid-20th century, lobotomies were hailed as breakthrough therapy.

Doctors assured families it would calm patients and restore order.

Thousands underwent the procedure, often without consent.

When results proved disastrous, critics were dismissed as alarmists.

Hospitals reframed failures as *"partial successes."*

Big Pharma Narratives

Pharmaceutical companies frame pricing as innovation:

"We need high prices to fund research."

Meanwhile, marketing budgets dwarf R&D.

Patients pay $600 for drugs that cost $6 to make.

The narrative gaslights by insisting the system is benevolent—

while profit margins tell another story.

Case Study · The Opioid Crisis

In the 1990s, drug companies launched campaigns claiming new opioid painkillers carried *"low risk of addiction."*

Sales reps repeated the line.

Ads reassured doctors.

Medical journals published sponsored studies downplaying risks.

When dependency surged, patients were blamed for *"pain sensitivity."*

Addiction wasn't the pill's design—it was the patient's weakness.

Decades later, lawsuits revealed the deception—after entire towns were hollowed out.

———

Public Health Messaging

During crises, health agencies walk a tightrope: reassure the public without panic.

But when guidance shifts—masks unnecessary, then required;

travel safe, then restricted—citizens feel gaslit.

Some shifts stemmed from new evidence.

Others from fear of admitting error.

Result: eroded trust.

People don't know whether to believe the science—or the story about the science.

Trust fractures the same way in the exam room.

Scripts change; choreography doesn't.

Authority speaks faster than understanding can catch up.

Informed consent often functions as theater:

patients signing dense forms under stress,

in language few understand.

The signature becomes the shield.

Consent, once proof of comprehension, now protects the institution.

Case Study · Thalidomide

In the 1950s and '60s, thalidomide was prescribed to pregnant women as a "safe" cure for morning sickness.

Ads praised its effectiveness.

When thousands of children were born with severe birth defects,

companies denied connection, then reframed it as *"rare complications."*

Truth emerged only after relentless investigation.

The episode revealed medical gaslighting on a mass scale:

harm minimized, evidence delayed, tragedy reframed until denial collapsed.

The lesson didn't end with recall.

It only changed form.

What was once corporate denial became clinical doubt—less visible, just as real.

Chronic Conditions and Invisible Illness

Patients with long-term or hard-to-measure conditions—fibromyalgia, chronic fatigue, long COVID—face a subtler gaslight:

"You're fine."

When tests come back normal, suffering is pathologized as personality.

Long COVID exposed this at scale—millions dismissed as anxious until data proved otherwise.

When symptoms defy the chart, belief becomes the first medicine.

Case Study · COVID-19 Vaccine Updates

In 2020–21, officials urged vaccination as *"the path back to normal."*

When breakthrough infections rose, framing shifted:

vaccines wouldn't prevent infection but would prevent severe illness.

Later, boosters became "essential for ongoing protection."

Each change reflected evolving science—

but communication often landed as contradiction.

For many, the story changed faster than the explanation.

Historical Case Study · Tuskegee

From 1932–1972, Black men with syphilis were studied without treatment—even after penicillin was available.

They were told they were receiving care.

Generations later, the legacy lingers: communities wary of medicine's promises.

For Tuskegee's survivors, trust never healed.

———

Tech in Medicine

AI diagnostic tools promise precision—and deliver bias.

In 2019, a major risk-assessment algorithm underestimated Black patients' needs

because it used past healthcare spending as a proxy for health.

Less money spent meant *less need*—

and entire populations were sidelined by code.

Apps track data, then quietly sell it.

Hospitals tout *"efficiency gains"* while wait times rise.

Framing: *"Cutting-edge care."*

Reality: patients become data points.

Gaslighting in Mental Health

Patients are told:

- "Others have it worse."
- "You just need to think positive."
- "That medication side effect isn't real."

Minimizing distress reframes pain as weakness.

The outcome: shame, not healing.

The Psychology of Medical Gaslighting

Why do patients accept dismissals that clash with experience?

- **Authority bias**—Doctors carry cultural authority; *"It's nothing to worry about"* overrides instinct.
- **Optimism bias**—People want to believe medicine is on their side; doubting the doctor feels scarier than doubting themselves.
- **Gender and racial bias**—Women's pain is systematically downplayed; minority patients receive less aggressive care for identical conditions.

Medical gaslighting works because it hijacks trust.

Patients want to believe.

That trust, when exploited, delays truth until damage is done.

- Document every symptom in your own words, not just the chart.
- Ask for evidence behind every "standard protocol."
- Get second opinions—then compare language, not just results.

In medicine, certainty comforts—
but humility saves lives.

PART IV
THE ENGINES
TECHNOLOGY, FAITH, AND
THE INDUSTRIES OF BELIEF

When lies move at light speed,
memory is the last defense.

The engines of modern life don't just move us forward.
They decide what we notice, what we fear,
and what we're told to believe.

From algorithms to pulpits, from markets to media,
each promises order—
and delivers obedience.

These are the gears that turn conviction into commerce,
belief into product,
and truth into something metered by subscription.

Global Prelude
Same fog, different systems

THE FOG DOESN'T STOP AT THE BORDER.

Freedom House's 2024 map showed a fourteenth straight year

of decline in online freedom—

twenty-seven nations sliding backward.

Different languages.

Same choreography.

In India, deepfakes blurred elections until rumor looked like report.

In Europe, TikTok turned politics into pulse—

proof that law still moves slower than code.

Authoritarian or democratic, the pattern holds:

speed outruns truth,

architecture outruns ethics.

The pipes differ—

WhatsApp in Mumbai,

Telegram in Tunis,

X in Texas—

but the water is the same grey.

Distortion isn't an export.

It's the native language of connectivity.

To write about gaslighting today

is to write about globalization's quiet twin—

synchronized confusion.

14
THE TECH TRAP
CONVENIENCE, CONTROL,
AND THE ILLUSION OF CHOICE

Technology promised transparency. It delivered reflection.

Algorithms don't argue—they curate.

The new oracle doesn't need faith, only data.

Your phone pings.

A notification appears: *"You might like this."*

You do.

That's the problem.

The algorithm already knows you.

It predicts your click before you think,

anticipates your anger before you feel it,

and serves your confirmation bias like room service.

You aren't using the app.
The app is using you.

————

Technology gaslights by reframing inconvenience as progress,

surveillance as personalization,

and control as freedom.

The Promise of Progress

Every upgrade is framed as improvement—faster, lighter, smarter—

but progress often carries trade-offs no one admits.

- Newer phones with fewer ports.
- Cloud storage that locks you in.
- *"Convenience"* that harvests more data.

Users are told: *"You're choosing innovation."*

Reality: the choice was never yours.

Ask anyone who tried to keep a headphone jack.

If it feels like an option, it probably isn't.

Terms of Service

Click *"I agree."*

You didn't read eighty-seven pages of legalese.

No one did.

Yet companies frame consent as informed.

When harm surfaces—privacy breaches, exploitative clauses—

you're told: *"You agreed."*

In 2018, it emerged that millions of Facebook profiles had been harvested without consent for political targeting.

The company framed it as a *"breach of trust"* by a third party.

But the platform's architecture—the system built to vacuum up data—was the real culprit.

Facebook said, *"We didn't sell your data."*

Reality: the platform was built so others could take it.

Surveillance as Service

"Your data helps us serve you better."

That's the pitch—and, to a point, it's true.

Maps guide you home faster.

Recommendations save you time.

Autocomplete finishes your thoughts.

But the same data builds a dossier that knows you better than you know yourself—

bedtime from scrolls, stress from typing rhythm, politics from the posts that make you pause.

In 2012, Facebook quietly ran an experiment on nearly 700 000 users, manipulating feeds to test whether emotions could be influenced at scale.

They could.

The study revealed what platforms do constantly:

test what keeps you engaged.

Surveillance, once the domain of states, now wears the smile of convenience.

Every *Allow Notifications?* pop-up is a small act of consent disguised as choice.

Historical Parallel · Loyalty Cards

Before platforms, grocery *"rewards"* normalized surveillance:

swipe for a discount, surrender your habits.

The pitch was savings.

The product was pattern recognition.

Tech simply scaled it—from bread to beliefs.

Once we traded privacy for pennies at checkout,

trading it for a feed felt natural.

Tech as Neutral (Except It Isn't)

- Social platforms claim to be *"just platforms,"* yet decide which voices rise.
- Search engines claim *"unbiased results,"* while algorithms privilege advertisers.
- Devices claim *"privacy settings,"* but default to maximum data sharing.

Neutrality has become the mask for control.

Case Study · The Trending Tab

"Trending" once sounded like consensus—until leaks showed human hands seeding and suppressing topics.

When Facebook removed editors and let the model run, fake stories spiked.

The gaslight wasn't the feed.

It was the illusion of neutrality behind it.

Case Study · TikTok's Algorithm

TikTok sells itself as pure entertainment—an endless stream *"just for you."*

But regulators and researchers warn: the algorithm doesn't reflect your interests; it shapes them.

Users report being funneled into rabbit holes—extreme dieting, political radicalization, conspiracy loops—within days.

The gaslight: *"We're only showing you what you like."*

Reality: the system decides what you like, then insists it was your choice all along.

The Feed as Mirror

We're told the feed reflects our interests.

It doesn't.

It edits the reflection before handing it back.

The system doesn't record your taste.

It manufactures it—then thanks you for the input.

The Filter Bubble

Algorithms personalize until reality fractures.

You and your neighbor search the same term and see different worlds—

each convinced theirs is the whole.

When curation replaces common ground,

facts don't vanish;

they just stop overlapping.

The Myth of Digital Ownership

What looks like convenience in design is often coercion in contract.

Click *buy*, and you lease.

When the server dies, so does your library.

Even death isn't an exception: most Terms of Service mark accounts *"non-transferable."*

Your *collection* dies with you.

The gaslight isn't that you lost something.

It's that you're told you never really had it.

That's the truth of the cloud: permanence is a performance.

Historical Parallel · The Music that Vanished

In 2019, millions of songs disappeared from MySpace after a botched server migration.

A decade of music—gone.

The illusion of permanence collapsed in an instant.

The same fragility haunts every cloud library.

You don't own the software; you rent it.

You don't own the music; you stream it.

Platforms sell this as *"flexibility."*

In reality, it's a trap of recurring revenue and vanishing autonomy.

The Engineered Life Cyle

What looks like innovation is often expiration with a new name.

Devices don't just fail.

They're designed to.

- Phones slow mysteriously before new models launch.
- Parts become unrepairable.
- *"Support"* ends early, nudging upgrades.

Apple admitted slowing older iPhones *"to protect batteries."*

Consumers saw something else: forced obsolescence sold as care.

The gaslight: *"We did this for your benefit."*

SURVEILLANCE REFRAMED

Surveillance now wears many disguises:

smart speakers that *help,*

fitness trackers that *empower,*

work laptops that *measure.*

The gaslight: *"We care. We trust. We protect."*

Reality: constant oversight.

THE POETIC TRUTH OF CLEAN WAR

Every generation promises a cleaner battlefield.

Cavalry gave way to artillery, artillery to air power, air power to drones, and drones to algorithms—each upgrade sold as moral progress.

That's the poetic truth of technology: salvation through precision.

"Smart." "Surgical." "Humane."

The adjectives multiply while the bodies stay the same.

Officials replay footage like confessionals, circling the target, swearing intent was pure.

The explanation becomes the absolution.

Machines don't just deliver payloads; they deliver innocence.

The goal isn't malice; it's control.

Innovation promises moral control, but every new interface moves the trigger farther from the conscience.

Counter-Moves · Autonomy as Absolution

Now the trigger belongs to code.

Autonomous systems identify and strike before conscience can intervene.

When civilians die, the headline reads: *System Error—Under Review.*

Responsibility dissolves in the circuitry.

Officials call it efficiency.

Engineers call it progress.

The public calls it peace of mind.

The issue isn't the machine.

It's the policy that hides behind it.

> *When no one pulls the trigger*
> *everyone feels innocent.*

The algorithm becomes the scapegoat.

And the machine—our most obedient servant—becomes our most convenient priest.

Case Study · The Cloud's Dirty Secret

Silicon Valley calls it dematerialization—the idea that moving life online saves the planet.

But the cloud isn't weightless.

Each data center draws the power of a small city and gulps water to stay cool.

AI models promise "green optimization" while emitting more carbon in training than five cars burn in a lifetime.

A phone that tracks your "sustainability goals" runs on lithium dug by hand and cobalt mined by children.

The new gospel of progress hides its cost behind a screen saver.

The Psychology of Tech Gaslighting

Why do users keep upgrading, scrolling, and agreeing?

- **FOMO bias**—Fear of missing out makes skipping upgrades feel risky.
- **Authority bias**—If Apple or Google says it's secure, most people defer.
- **Learned helplessness**—After enough unread Terms of Service, people stop questioning.
- **Normalization bias**—When privacy erodes slowly, we adapt.
- **Illusion of choice**—Endless toggles hide that the core trade-off —data for access—never changes.

Tech gaslighting doesn't hide flaws.

It exhausts resistance.

It doesn't erase options.

It buries them under fatigue.

The Dopamine Economy

Every notification is a slot machine.

Every like, a hit.

The platform doesn't want you informed.

It wants you engaged.

Engagement is the product,

attention the currency,

outrage the fuel.

Outrage scrolls better than calm.

Anxiety refreshes faster than peace.

Former Facebook executive Chamath Palihapitiya admitted:

> *"The short-term, dopamine-driven feedback loops we've created are destroying how society works."*

Sean Parker, Facebook's first president, added:

> *"The goal was to consume as much user time as possible. God only knows what it's doing to our children's brains."*

Intermittent reward creates craving.

Frictionless reward creates tolerance.

When the screen dims,

the mind twitches for proof of connection.

Echoes and Oversight

Lawmakers summon tech CEOs to televised hearings.

Executives promise audits, publish new terms—Integrity teams, Trust systems.

It's the oldest procedural gaslight:

procedure as performance.

The spectacle soothes outrage

while preserving architecture.

- **Curate deliberately**—unfollow, mute, unsubscribe. The default feed is control, not choice.
- **Create friction**—set limits, use timers, break the loop. Attention is a resource, not a reflex.
- **Diversify inputs**—if your feed agrees with you perfectly, you're in a bubble.
- **Read contracts, not buttons**—clicks disguise terms.
- **Ask what happens when the device fails**—who holds the power?
- **Audit ownership**—if you can't sell it, pass it down, or repair it, you don't own it.

The story isn't that you use the app.

It's that the app uses you.

Devices script attention.

The economy scripts obedience.

> *When the product is free,*
> *you're not the customer—*
> *you're the product.*

Digital Amnesia

Screens store everything, but recall is hollow.

The more we save, the less we remember.

Our memories shrink to match the search bar.

That's the quiet trick of the digital age:

we forget faster because we know it's saved somewhere else.

Algorithmic Distortion

Two decades ago we blamed the feed for what we clicked.

Now we blame it for what we can't escape.

In Germany's 2025 election, even blank accounts drew partisan feeds within days.

The algorithm doesn't wait for belief.

It builds it.

Neutrality, in the digital age, is only the first stage of targeting.

Every swipe is a signal.

Every pause is a confession.

Every reaction becomes code.

The algorithm doesn't serve truth.

It serves engagement.

Outrage pays better than proportion.

A study of Facebook's election feed found that emotion—not accuracy—decides what survives.

The louder the pulse, the longer the stay.

And here's the paradox:

even when the content isn't extreme,

the system keeps nudging you toward what holds you.

Knowing the loop doesn't free you from it.

It only names the cage.

Distortion has moved from message to mechanism.

The lie isn't in the story—it's in the structure.

Clarity, in this world,

is learning to read the code

beneath the scroll.

Closing Reflection

The machine was built to remember us.

Yet it quietly teaches us to forget ourselves.

We scroll; it studies.

We pause; it predicts.

Somewhere between those gestures, authorship shifts.

But the same lens that edits can also illuminate.

The lamp in your pocket can still turn outward—

not as spotlight, but as lantern.

The question isn't whether the machine gaslights.

It's whether we'll keep letting its glow decide what deserves to be
seen.

Every feed is a hall of mirrors.

The only real choice is whether you keep looking for the frame—

or the courage to step outside it.

Control doesn't end with code; it just changes currency—

from data to dollars.

15

THE INSURANCE ILLUSION

PROTECTION THAT VANISHES WHEN IT'S NEEDED MOST

Every promise of protection carries fine print—and every clause is written in smoke. Premiums rise. Coverage shrinks. Promises stay the same.

———

The flames came fast.

A dry wind carried embers across the canyon like sparks from a forge, igniting rooftops in seconds.

Families scrambled to pack bags and grab photo albums.

Fire trucks raced in, but the blaze was bigger, hotter, faster than any hoses could handle.

By morning, entire neighborhoods lay in ashes.

The Johnsons thought they had done everything right.

They'd paid premiums for twenty-seven years.

Their policy binder sat neatly in a fireproof safe.

Insurance, after all, was the guarantee—the quiet promise that if disaster struck, someone would help rebuild.

But when they called, desperate and dazed, the voice on the other end didn't sound like rescue.

"I'm sorry," the adjuster said flatly. "Your policy was terminated six months ago. Increased wildfire risk. A notice was sent."

The Johnsons were left with rubble—and the gaslight that they should have known better.

———

The Gaslight of Risk

Insurance sells itself as the ultimate security blanket—you pay, we protect.

But this promise was always conditional, long before the Johnsons discovered it the hard way.

The fine print tells another story.

When wildfires sweep through California, Colorado, or Hawaii, entire communities learn the same lesson: the system that promised protection can vanish overnight.

Insurers quietly withdraw from regions, citing "unsustainable risk."

Premiums skyrocket. Coverage evaporates.

The deception starts with the frame, not the facts.

Companies call these withdrawals "responsible business decisions" or even "in the best interests of the community."

Ads still show happy families, rebuilt homes, reassuring slogans.

Reality is abandonment—betrayal disguised as prudence.

It's not that insurers can't pay.

It's that they don't want to.

THE POETIC TRUTH OF PROTECTION

Every insurance commercial is a poem about safety.

"Like a good neighbor."

"You're in good hands."

"Nationwide is on your side."

These lines aren't actuarial—they're emotional.

They trade in trust, familiarity, comfort.

They sell the feeling of being cared for—even loved.

But in the real world, coverage decisions are made by algorithms and risk models.

If your house sits in the wrong zip code—wildfire-prone, flood-prone, hurricane-prone—that "good neighbor" may move out of town.

If your risk profile doesn't fit profitability, those "good hands" let go.

The poetic truth remains: you thought you were buying safety.

What you bought was an illusion.

INVISIBLE DAMAGE, VISIBLE DENIAL

Wildfire smoke doesn't stop at the property line.

It seeps through vents, coats insulation, lingers in clothes and lungs.

Yet when families file claims for smoke or soot contamination, adjusters often call the damage "cosmetic."

The roof survived—therefore the house survived.

Tests show something different: microscopic particulates embedding in drywall, HVAC filters blackened with toxins, carpets that test positive for heavy metals.

The harm is invisible until the coughs start.

But invisibility is useful. It lets the company pretend the disaster is over.

California's insurer of last resort still denies many smoke claims even after court rulings against it.

The argument? That smoke isn't structural damage—it's atmosphere.

That semantic dodge saves billions.

The family pays the cleanup; the insurer keeps the slogan.

When destruction hides at the molecular level, language becomes the barricade.

"Surface residue." "Airborne particulates." "Temporary odor."

Words written to shrink reality until it fits the balance sheet.

Engines and Denial

It isn't only homes. The same gaslight idles in the driveway.

In nearly every state, auto insurance isn't a choice—it's the price of admission to the road.

You pay a corporation before you can move.

The promise of freedom runs on mandated dependence.

Drivers are told rates reflect performance—tickets, collisions, responsibility.

But increasingly the variables have nothing to do with how you drive.

Algorithms score your risk by zip code, credit history, even job title.

Live in the wrong neighborhood or carry debt, and you're a "higher risk," even with a spotless record.

The company calls it *data-driven fairness.*

A man in Dallas renews his policy online.

The system adds fifty dollars a month without explanation.

The agent blames "updated underwriting models."

He's never filed a claim.

He moved one block—across a boundary the algorithm doesn't like.

That's the hidden exchange—citizenship for compliance.

The state requires coverage; the insurer defines the cost.

The freedom to drive becomes the freedom to subsidize risk calculations you'll never see.

When Protection Becomes Denial

Then there's the final promise—the one meant to last beyond you.

Life insurance: the quiet pact between caution and love.

You pay so your family won't have to.

But the contract has escape hatches.

Most policies include a *contestability period*—usually two years—during which the company can cancel or deny if it discovers "misstatements."

A missed blood-pressure reading, an unreported prescription, a forgotten doctor's visit.

Even honest mistakes can become grounds for refusal.

A widow files a claim six months after her husband's death.

The insurer delays, requests more records, then denies.

The reason—he failed to disclose a "pre-existing condition": mild asthma noted once, ten years earlier.

The premiums were current. The denial arrived two weeks after the funeral.

Exclusions multiply—suicide, "risky activity," "death while intoxicated."'

The language expands until nearly any misfortune can be recast as disqualification.

The ultimate irony: the more faithfully you pay, the less likely you are to challenge.

Grief softens resistance.

Beneficiaries rarely fight corporations while burying loved ones.

In theory, life insurance is incontestable after the first two years.

In practice, delays and reinterpretations achieve the same effect.

The protection meant to outlive you becomes another conversation about what counts as "real."

A check that never comes.

A policy that never pays.

A voice on the phone that still says, "We're here for you."

When Protection Becomes Predation

The cruelest twist is timing.

Policies often terminate—or premiums spike—right after major disasters.

A hurricane hits Florida—rates triple.

A pandemic strikes—business coverage suddenly excludes pandemics.

Moments of greatest need become moments of greatest withdrawal.

And yet the ads roll on: gentle voices, soothing promises, reassuring metaphors—

while contracts evolve to protect the insurer, not the insured.

THE BIGGER PICTURE

Insurance isn't just an industry.

It's a metaphor.

It preys on our deepest longing—certainty in an uncertain world.

That longing makes us vulnerable to the very contracts designed to betray it.

THE FINAL BETRAYAL

When the Johnsons stood in the ruins of their home, the shock wasn't only the fire.

It was realizing the protection they thought they had was never really there.

The adjuster's voice was just the final blow.

"We're sorry. Your policy no longer applies."

COUNTER-MOVES · POLICYHOLDERS

- Record every promise—calls, emails, policy changes.
- Ask the payout question first—"Under what condition will this not apply?"
- Compare marketing language to the contract. Treat the gap as truth.

You pay to be safe. You trust to be secure.

And just when you need it most,

you're told you should have known better.

16

THE SPECTACLE

GAMES, FAME, AND THE FOG OF ENTERTAINMENT

A press conference.

NFL executives face the cameras: "We have no evidence concussions cause long-term damage."

The gaslight wasn't just denial.

It was the story that bone-crushing hits built character—not dementia.

The poetic truth was toughness.
The reality was brain damage.

———

The same cameras that turned politics into performance now turn sport into sermon.

THE NFL · DENIAL IN HELMETS

For years, the league buried studies linking repeated concussions to CTE.

Its *Mild Traumatic Brain Injury Committee*, formed in 1994, issued papers downplaying any connection between head blows and long-term harm.

Players were told headaches were "just part of the game."

Trainers patched them up and sent them back out.

The myth of invincibility stayed intact.

Meanwhile, stars like Mike Webster and Junior Seau deteriorated—brains ravaged by trauma, families grieving while the league repeated: "No proven link."

Denial was cheaper than reform.

Silence easier than change.

Protect the shield, not the science.

The gaslight wasn't just a lie.

It was armor that bought the NFL decades of silence—while stadiums roared and TV billions flowed.

The NCAA · Amateurism as Virtue

For decades, the NCAA wrapped itself in purity: *"Student first, athlete second."*

Scholarships were portrayed as payment enough while billion-dollar March Madness contracts and jersey sales piled up.

The poetic truth was noble sacrifice for education.

The reality was unpaid labor fueling an empire.

Even with new NIL (Name, Image, Likeness) rules, the framing persists.

A few stars earn millions; most still grind for nothing.

In 2021, the Supreme Court's ruling in *NCAA v. Alston* stripped away the moral veil.

Justice Brett Kavanaugh wrote:

> *"The NCAA's business model would be flatly illegal in almost any other industry in America."*

The gaslight: calling exploitation tradition.

CASE STUDY · FAIRNESS REDEFINED

Sport was once the last honest arena—numbers, times, and weight classes that didn't care who you were, only what you could do.

Now fairness itself is being rewritten.

Governing bodies have redrawn the rules, allowing athletes born male to compete in women's divisions.

The new vocabulary followed: *inclusion, gender-affirming, authentic identity.*

The premise—that biology no longer matters—became the story institutions asked everyone to repeat.

Coaches who question it, risk discipline.

Female athletes who object are labeled intolerant.

Parents who speak up are told they're endangering their children's futures.

And anyone who asks about muscle mass, bone density, or safety learns the quickest way to end a conversation: be called *phobic.*

That's poetic truth at work—a story that *feels* compassionate while demanding denial of what's visible.

Riley Gaines, an All-American swimmer, described sharing a locker room with a biological male competitor.

Her statement wasn't inflammatory; it was descriptive.

Yet the reaction proved the point: witnesses were shamed for seeing what they saw.

The governing message was simple—*you're not supposed to notice.*

And if you do, *you're the problem.*

The language of equality—once rooted in recognition of difference—now erases the very boundaries that made women's sports possible.

When biology becomes negotiable, fairness becomes metaphor.

When outcomes replace merit, competition becomes theater.

Gaslighting tells the audience that resistance is cruelty and silence is virtue.

But truth isn't cruelty.

It's respect—for effort, for limits, for reality itself.

Olympics and Abuse

The Olympic ideal promised protection.

Coaches told young gymnasts that pain was discipline, cruelty the price of greatness.

When survivors of Larry Nassar's abuse finally spoke, the narrative shattered—revealing a system that prized medals over children.

Reports showed USA Gymnastics and Michigan State ignored credible complaints for years.

Reputation mattered more than safety.

At sentencing, Aly Raisman said:

 *"You convinced my parents you were the doctor who cared for amazing athletes. You abused that trust."*

Hollywood's Stage

For decades, the casting couch was sold as opportunity.

Harvey Weinstein and others cloaked predation in mentorship: *"I can make you a star."*

The industry whispered, *"That's just how it works."*

Careers died if silence broke.

The gaslight wasn't just Weinstein.

It was an ecosystem that normalized exploitation as tradition.

Music's Contracts of Captivity

The stage lights promised freedom; the contracts delivered chains.

Artists signed "paths to immortality" that locked away masters, names, and royalties.

Prince scrawled *slave* on his face.

Taylor Swift re-recorded albums to reclaim her work.

The poetic truth was creative freedom.
The reality was servitude,
signed in ink and celebrated in lights.

The Vanishing Contributor

When power falls, institutions rewrite the record.

Credits vanish. Photos crop. Histories soften.

The gaslight: *"They were never that important."*

Erasure doesn't undo influence—it warns others that legacy is conditional.

Soviet editors airbrushed Trotsky from photos.

Hollywood does the same—digitally.

Acknowledging both truth and wrongdoing isn't contradiction.

It's honesty.

Historical Parallel · Gladiators

Rome promised bread and circuses—unity through spectacle.

Crowds cheered while men were thrown to lions.

The poetic truth was national pride.

The reality was disposable lives sacrificed for distraction.

That lineage is unbroken—from blood-soaked arenas to billion-dollar stadiums, from Hollywood backlots to Super Bowl halftime shows.

The gaslight never changes:

The show unites us. So don't ask about the cost.

> *When the show must go on,*
> *the truth must go quiet.*

The Psychology of the Game

Why do these gaslights work?

- **Hero worship**—Fans need their idols invincible.
- **Normalization**—Pain reframed as tradition.
- **Distraction**—Spectacle cloaks exploitation.
- **Suspension of disbelief**—The story tastes better than the truth.
- **Escapism**—The game promises relief, even as it deepens the wounds we ignore.

The Moral Myth of Spectacle

Every era turns its distractions into moral theater.

Rome called it unity. Hollywood calls it representation. The NFL calls it brotherhood.

The narrative isn't just that the show must go on—it's that watching the show redeems us.

Buy the ticket, wear the jersey, post the hashtag—you've participated in virtue.

That's the poetic truth: distraction disguised as duty.

The crowd believes their cheers sanctify the system.

Gaslighting by applause—pain reframed as progress, harm recast as heroism, all wrapped in lights and music.

When the lights fade, the stadium quiets, and the credits roll, the illusion doesn't end.

It resets—waiting for the next story to sell comfort disguised as conscience.

The Economy of Illusion

Spectacle isn't just an escape. It's an economy.

Every click, view, and ticket keeps the machine humming.

Fans call it loyalty. Investors call it engagement. Psychologists call it conditioning.

The outcome's the same: devotion becomes data.

Poetic truth sells better than reality because it flatters the buyer.

Every fan becomes a moral shareholder in the myth—a tiny piece of righteousness for the price of attention.

———

The Audience Contract

Every gaslight needs applause.

The lie only works if the crowd keeps clapping.

Spectacle sells two tickets—one for escape, and one for consent.

The viewer trades agency for awe, truth for tribe.

We cheer men who break their bodies for our weekends.

We stream shows that moralize the same vices they glamorize.

We hashtag outrage in the morning and binge the sequel that night.

You don't have to lie to the audience if you can make them enjoy the illusion.

Poetic truth becomes a loyalty program.

Each purchase says, *I know it's fake—but I like how it feels.*

The stadium isn't just a venue.

It's a cathedral where faith is measured in volume, not virtue.

And when belief gets loud enough, even the scoreboard starts to look sacred.

Counter-Moves · Watching the Scoreboard

- Ask: Who profits most? Who pays the cost?
- Track the gap between the highlight reel and the hospital bill.

The lights fade, the crowd goes home, and the machine resets.

Tomorrow there's a new game, a new film, a new cause to prove we still believe.

The names change; the transaction doesn't.

Every empire runs on stories that make the suffering look noble.

Every audience learns to cheer for its own anesthesia.

That's the cost of poetic truth at scale.

It never asks for clarity—only attention.

When applause becomes prayer,
faith follows the spotlight.

17

THE GOSPEL OF POWER

WHEN REVERENCE MEETS POWER—AND POWER WINS

S unday morning.

The pews fill.

A preacher declares: *"We welcome everyone."*

Minutes later, the sermon names who doesn't belong.

Congregants nod—some uneasily.

The official message: love and inclusion.

The subtext: boundaries and exclusion.

Faith offers comfort,

but it also wields story as power.

And when story becomes unquestionable,

it risks becoming gaslight.

———

The Double Message of Faith

Religions often preach paradoxes:

- *Come as you are*—but change to fit.
- *God is love*—but God condemns you.
- *All are equal*—but some must stay silent.

Contradictions framed as mysteries can deepen devotion—

or dissolve trust.

When paradox becomes a weapon,

faith turns to fog.

Ask anyone who's sat through a sermon that promised welcome while naming the unwelcome—the haze isn't metaphor.

It's felt in the room.

History Rewritten in Doctrine

Sacred texts have passed through centuries of translation and debate.

Communities are told, *"This is how it has always been taught,"* even when records reveal layers of councils, revisions, and interpretation.

The gaslight comes when genuine debate is erased to create the illusion of eternal uniformity.

Authority and Infallibility

Across traditions, dissent is often framed as rebellion against God rather than disagreement with human interpretation.

Abuse scandals show how institutions reframe harm as rumor, loyalty, or *discipline.*

Survivors are told their pain is rumor, their memory rebellion, their scars misunderstanding.

Reform as Reverence

Critiquing hypocrisy isn't an attack on faith—it's a defense of it.

Prophets of every tradition spoke truth to their own institutions,

not because they despised them,

but because they loved them enough to demand honesty.

The gaslight isn't always inside the sanctuary.

When faith is dismissed as *backward* by cultural elites,

believers face a quieter fog—

the assumption that intellect and devotion can't coexist.

Real faith holds both.

Case Study · The Prosperity Gospel

Some modern preachers promise: *"Faith will make you rich."*

When believers stay poor, the blame shifts: *"You didn't believe enough."*

The doctrine reframes systemic poverty as personal failure while enriching the pulpit.

When faith becomes monetized,

doubt becomes subscription.

Gaslighting in Ritual

- **Confession** reframed as control: *"If you don't reveal everything, you're unclean."*
- **Sacrifice** reframed as proof of devotion instead of compassion.
- **Silence** reframed as virtue, even when it conceals abuse.

Ritual can heal—

or it can hide.

Case Study · The Inquisition

During the Spanish Inquisition, faith and power fused until questioning became heresy.

Ordinary people were accused, coerced, and paraded as proof of "purity."

The gaslight wasn't just torture—

it was the insistence that fear was faith,

suffering sanctification,

silence safety.

The Inquisition shows how institutions weaponize fear;

Jonestown shows what happens when fear hardens into obedience.

Case Study · Jonestown (1978)

Jim Jones built a utopia in Guyana by preaching equality and belonging.

Followers believed they were escaping corruption.

But dissent became betrayal.

Families who questioned were told they lacked faith.

When tragedy came—more than 900 deaths—it was reframed as *"revolutionary suicide."*

A final gaslight that twisted murder into devotion.

Interfaith Narratives

Religions sometimes gaslight each other—

portraying rivals as *"cults,"*

rewriting history to claim continuity of dominance,

or dismissing others' miracles as delusion.

Believers caught between narratives begin to doubt not God,

but themselves.

Personal Experience vs. Institutional Narrative

Many believers describe spiritual witness—moments of peace, prayer, revelation.

Yet when those experiences diverge from the official line, they're dismissed or reframed.

A prayerful prompting becomes *"just emotion."*

A doubt becomes *"a temptation."*

When lived faith is recast as mistake,

dependence replaces conviction.

Healthy faith seeks balance—

listening to conscience while sustaining trusted leadership.

Faith as Political Weapon

When faith and politics merge, narratives shift fast:

- Wars reframed as *"holy."*
- Policies reframed as *"moral duty."*
- Leaders reframed as *"chosen by God."*

The gaslight works by turning disagreement into heresy.

When faith crowns politics,

dissent becomes sin.

The Moral Truth

When theology merges with ideology, creed turns into campaign.

Political leaders borrow the vocabulary of salvation—*redemption, calling, destiny*—to frame agendas as divine missions.

That's poetic truth weaponized: language that feels sacred while serving strategy.

Gaslighting begins when doubt itself becomes immoral.

Citizens are told that questioning policy is questioning God.

The pulpit becomes podium, and the sermon becomes slogan.

Faith loses nothing by humility.

It loses everything by certainty that sanctifies power.

The Psychology of Religious Gaslighting

Why do people accept contradictions in faith more easily than in other parts of life?

- **Sacred framing**—When words are declared holy, skepticism sleeps.
- **Fear of exile**—Questioning risks losing family, community, eternity.
- **Reverence for tradition**—Heritage makes doubt feel like betrayal.
- **Cognitive dissonance**—When promises don't align with reality, memory bends to protect belief.

Religious gaslighting thrives not on gullibility,

but on the stakes: belonging, purpose, salvation.

- **Protect personal revelation**—test it against scripture, conscience, and enduring truth.
- **Anchor to conscience**—even when institutions deny it.
- **Compare teachings with outcomes**—does the fruit match the promise?
- **Watch for monetization**—when belief becomes transaction.

Mini-Case · The Split Screen

Cognitive dissonance is the strain of holding two contradictory truths.

Rather than resolve the contradiction, many bend reality until it fits:

- A leader exposed in scandal is reframed as *"tested but chosen."*
- A failing policy becomes *"proof it wasn't tried hard enough."*
- A personal doubt becomes *"a test of faith."*

The tension between what we see and what we want to believe

creates fertile ground for gaslighting.

The brightest lights—spotlights, slogans, certainty—

are often the ones that drown doubt.

When the cost of admitting error feels higher than the cost of distortion,

dissonance wins.

The task of every believer is to guard the lantern—

so the flame of faith is never swallowed by fog.

True faith illuminates.
Distorted faith deceives.

The line between them isn't drawn in scripture.

It's drawn in practice—

where power meets humility.

And at the edges of belief—where power refuses explanation—the unbelievable begins to look familiar.

The stories exiled as fantasy often return as evidence.

Part V
Private Realities
How the fog moves through family, identity, and daily life

*The smallest lamp
can outshine the thickest fog.*

Public distortions are easy to see.
Private ones are harder.

Gaslighting becomes most intimate
when it hides inside love, language, and habit—
when it sounds like care, looks like comfort,
and feels like home.

These are the personal mirrors of distortion:
identity, family, technology, and time itself—
the places where we stop noticing the fog
because we've learned to breathe it.

Before distortion reaches the mirror,
it travels through imagination—
the borderland where belief fills
the gaps left by silence.

18

THE FRINGE EFFECT
WHEN THE UNBELIEVABLE
BECOMES UNDENIABLE

The lights in the sky have always drawn us upward.

The tunnel at the end of life has always pulled us inward.

And sometimes, something as simple as a children's book title throws us sideways.

These are the places where the "fringe" lives—at least that's what we've been told.

UFOs. Near-death experiences. The Mandela Effect.

They're the stories we laugh about, dismiss, or whisper late at night— just far enough outside polite conversation that mentioning them at the wrong dinner party feels risky.

And yet, each of them refuses to go away.

They endure because they force the same unsettling question:

When official narratives, scientific explanations, and personal experience collide—who decides what counts as real?

This isn't conspiracy hunting.

The pattern of labeling inconvenient observations as hallucinations.

The pattern of watching institutions tell us one thing for decades, only to pivot without apology.

If gaslighting is denying what someone saw, reframing what they felt, and repeating it until they doubt themselves—

then the so-called fringe isn't an outlier at all.

It's the perfect case study.

UAPs · From Weather Balloons to Congressional Hearings

In 1947, Roswell set the template: a disc one day, a weather balloon the next.

Every sighting since was explained away with phrases like *swamp gas, Venus on the horizon,* or *optical illusion.*

Mainstream media portrayed believers as cranks with shaky cameras.

Governments not only denied the phenomenon—they mocked it.

The ridicule was strategic: narrative control.

By branding interest in UFOs as unserious, institutions controlled the conversation without ever proving their case.

Then came 2017. *The New York Times* ran "Glowing Auras and 'Black Money': The Pentagon's Mysterious U.F.O. Program."

Declassified footage showed Navy pilots chasing objects moving in ways no known aircraft could.

Suddenly, the language shifted.

No longer *UFOs* but *UAPs—unidentified aerial phenomena.*

A rebrand that made the subject sound less like a tabloid headline and more like a policy memo.

The choreography is familiar:

- Decades of denial.
- A wall of ridicule.
- A partial admission—carefully worded, carefully staged.

The effect is subtle but corrosive: we learn that what was "crazy" can become "credible" overnight—

but only when the right people decide it's safe to believe.

The truth is out there, The X-Files told us.

What it didn't say is how easily those in power decide when we're allowed to look.

———

NDEs · Between Science and the Light

If UAPs challenge our skies, near-death experiences challenge our souls.

Millions across cultures describe strikingly similar visions:

floating above their bodies, moving through a tunnel, meeting a being of light, feeling peace beyond words.

Many return with uncanny knowledge—describing surgical tools they couldn't have seen, recounting conversations while unconscious.

Yet mainstream science calls NDEs hallucinations from oxygen loss, neurochemical surge, or cultural script.

The language is clinical, reductive, final: *what you think you saw wasn't real.*

In 1975, psychiatrist Raymond Moody gave these visions a name.

The debate never closed.

Hospitals file them as anecdotes; scientists reach for chemistry.

But Moody's work cracked a door that's never been shut.

The pattern repeats:

Experience gaslit by explanation.

Testimony brushed off as neural misfire.

Even skeptics concede one fact: NDEs change lives.

People return less afraid of death, more focused on meaning.

That's poetic truth in action—the story about death shaping how we live,

whether science approves or not.

Once again, testimony meets the scalpel: explained, dismissed, re-filed.

———

THE MANDELA EFFECT · WHEN MEMORY REBELS

If UAPs stretch the sky and NDEs stretch the soul,

the Mandela Effect stretches something more fragile—shared memory.

Thousands swore they remembered Nelson Mandela dying in prison in the 1980s.

They recalled the coverage, the mourning, the widow's speech.

But Mandela lived until 2013.

Then came others: *Berenstain* remembered as *Berenstein*.

"Luke, I am your father" instead of "No, I am your father."

These aren't quirky errors.

They're shared certainties that never were.

The response is predictable—ridicule, laughter, dismissal.

Your memory is faulty. You're imagining things. Everyone knows it's Berenstain.

But the Mandela Effect exposes the heart of gaslighting:

What happens when you know you saw something—

and the record says otherwise?

What happens when millions share that same *wrong* memory?

It suggests gaslighting isn't only external.

It may be woven into perception itself.

The Matrix captured it in one scene: Neo sees a black cat twice.

Déjà vu, he's told, is a glitch in the system.

The moment stuck because it rang true—

what if reality is stitched together by fragile seams?

The Mandela Effect isn't just about faulty recall.

It's about the trust we place in our senses—

and how easily that trust can be turned against us.

The laugh track replaces rebuttal.

Once you're the punchline, your evidence never gets a hearing.

Once again, the record insists: memory is the liar.

Ancient Knowledge · Buried, Forgotten, or Suppressed?

If our memories can be gaslit, so can our timelines.

Not all mysteries are modern. Some are buried in dirt.

Göbekli Tepe in Turkey—an archaeological site dating back 12,000 years—rewrote human chronology.

For decades, anyone suggesting advanced cultures before Mesopotamia was ridiculed as fringe.

Then one excavation shifted the timeline overnight.

Or consider flood myths told from Mesopotamia to Mesoamerica— dismissed as folklore until geology found evidence of Ice-Age cataclysms.

For generations, "lost civilization" talk meant exile from academia.

Then the earth itself started to argue back.

Ridicule, then reluctant recalibration —
the oldest scientific ritual.

Gaslighting here isn't always malice—it's inertia.

Institutions protect paradigms.

But the effect is the same:

ideas branded *pseudo-science* can become *breakthrough discovery* overnight—no apology offered.

The Larger Pattern · Why the Fringe Matters

These stories may seem unrelated:

a pilot chasing lights,

a patient seeing the tunnel,

a child remembering the "wrong" cartoon,

a forgotten temple rewriting history.

The fringe isn't marginal.

It's the edge of perception—

the place where the machinery of gaslighting is most visible.

When governments, scientists, or institutions tell us that what we saw, felt, or remembered isn't real,

they aren't just dismissing data.

They're defining reality's borders.

The strangest thing about the fringe is how familiar it feels.

That's the tell: what looks like tinfoil today

often reads like tomorrow's press release.

The same sequence repeats—deny, ridicule, reframe, repeat.

The question isn't whether the truth is out there, in there, or back there.

It's why we're told to look away.

When institutions mock what they can't explain, individuals start questioning what they've been taught to see.

And once the outer mysteries crack, the inner ones—the self, the mirror—demand their turn.

19

THE DISTORTED REFLECTION

LABELS THAT SHRINK THE SELF

I dentity used to be description.

Now it's performance.

———

The classroom hums with introductions.

A student says, "I like math."

The teacher smiles: *"Really? Most girls don't say that."*

The words land like a label.

The room laughs.

One sentence later, she doubts herself.

Later, in a corporate training session, an employee says, "I don't think identity defines everything."

The facilitator replies, *"That perspective ignores lived experience."*

The message is clear: the label comes before the person.

Identity isn't just discovered.

It's assigned—and defended.

And when culture, institutions, or peers insist your lived reality doesn't align with the *official story,*

selfhood becomes the gaslight's casualty.

———

The Frame of Labels

Labels offer shorthand—but they also trap.

- "You're the funny one."
- "You're the quiet one."
- "You're not leadership material."

Once repeated, labels become cages.

Question them, and you're told: *"That's just who you are."*

Historical Parallel · Witch Trials

In Salem, women accused of witchcraft faced a trap: denial became proof of guilt.

"That's what a witch would say," judges declared.

Their own testimony was reframed against them.

The lesson was cruel but lasting—labels can override evidence, even self-defense.

- A woman speaks in a meeting—told she's *"too emotional."* (A man says the same—praised as *"passionate."*)
- Boys are told to *"man up"* and also to *"be sensitive."* (A contradiction no one can win.)
- Those who don't fit cultural scripts—whether in dress, belief, or behavior—hear: *"It's just a phase."*

Doubt imposed long enough becomes identity.

Cultural and Racial Frames

Communities face constant reframing:

- Concerns dismissed: *"Are you sure that really happened?"*
- Achievement discounted: *"You didn't earn this—it was handed to you."*
- History softened until struggle looks like progress.

Gaslighting doesn't always deny identity outright.

Sometimes it trims it—reducing the edges that don't fit the script.

Conservative identities face the mirror image:

labels like *"privileged," "out of touch,"* or *"backward"* used as shorthand to dismiss entire viewpoints.

The tactic cuts both ways.

Shrink complex people into caricatures and you never have to engage their ideas.

Identity gaslighting works in every direction; it reduces humanity to tribe.

Micro-Agressions and Safe Spaces

The new moral vocabulary of harm expands endlessly—micro-aggressions, lived experience, safe spaces.

What began as empathy now functions as orthodoxy: speech policed not by intent but by interpretation.

In classrooms and workplaces alike, discomfort is recast as danger.

The result isn't safety—it's fragility.

An emotional economy where disagreement itself is treated as violence.

And when every word is potential harm, silence feels like virtue.

The Immigrant Story

Immigrants live a double bind.

In their adopted country: *"You're not really from here."*

In their homeland: *"You've forgotten your roots."*

Belonging becomes conditional.

Identity, perpetual probation.

The Body as Billboard

- Eating disorders thrive on contradictions: *"Love yourself—but look like this."*
- *Wellness* reframed as control.
- Beauty standards shift, but shame remains constant—gaslighting by moving target.

Family Scripts

Sometimes the deepest gaslights come from home:

- *"We never fight."* (You remember shouting.)
- *"We gave you everything."* (You recall neglect.)
- *"You're imagining things."* (You hold scars.)

Families can rewrite the past so forcefully that children doubt their own childhoods—

rewriting not just events, but the child themself.

The Authenticity Trap

"Just be yourself."

It sounds liberating—until you try.

The moment your *self* disappoints someone's expectation, the script flips:

"That's not the real you."

Authenticity becomes performance, measured by approval.

You're authentic when others say you are.

Step outside the role, and you're *"confused."*

The gaslight: freedom with conditions.

Philosopher Charles Taylor called it the *ethic of authenticity—*

the demand to find your "true self" even when that self needs an audience to exist.

The irony: authenticity marketed as individuality still demands conformity.

Case Study · Britney Spears Conservatorship

For over a decade, Britney Spears said she was capable of managing her life.

Courts and family insisted otherwise.

Despite her performances and success, the label *"unfit"* held.

The gaslight was institutional: her lived reality was recast as delusion, and the label became law.

The Self-Help Industry

Books and podcasts sell poetic truths as laws of life:

- "Visualize it and it will happen."
- "Hustle harder."
- "You are enough"—until the next product tells you you're not.

The gaslight isn't failure.

It's the story that failure proves you were never enough to begin with.

Case Study · Leaving the Script

For people whose private lives don't match cultural or religious expectations,

gaslighting often sounds like:

- *"You're confused."*
- *"It's a phase."*
- *"You'll grow out of it."*

The result isn't only judgment—it's erosion of trust in your own desires, memories, and feelings.

That's why people walk away—from families, jobs, even faith—

because the reflection was scripted, not seen.

Gaslighting doesn't just distort facts.

It bends the mirror.

The Social Mirror

Identity online is curated, filtered, branded.

But the pressure to maintain a version of self that fits the cultural script gaslights people into believing their real life doesn't measure up.

Likes and shares become proof of existence.

The Collapse of Common Ground

When identity becomes the highest truth, empathy becomes negotiation.

Every conversation turns into translation between private languages.

Disagreement stops being debate and becomes offense.

The collective "we" fractures into curated "me's."

That's poetic truth turned inward—feelings elevated above facts until reality itself feels personal.

Gaslighting no longer needs an institution; it lives inside perception.

Without something shared beneath our differences, even honesty becomes relative.

The Psychology of Identity

Why do labels and frames sink so deep?

- **Authority of culture**—If "everyone says" you're X, it carries weight.
- **Need for belonging**—We accept labels to avoid exile.
- **Repetition effect**—A nickname repeated since childhood feels permanent, even when it never fit.

Gaslighting doesn't need to prove its case.

It only needs repetition—until you stop objecting.

- Keep a private archive—photos, journals, records of who you are.
- Refuse imposed labels that don't match your reality.
- Anchor identity in reflection, not reaction.
- Name the script—saying out loud, *"That's a label, not me,"* breaks its spell.

Every label is a mirror.

Clarity begins when you decide where to look.

Once you trust that mirror,

no label can rewrite your story.

> *The self that survives gaslighting*
> *is the one that keeps its own receipts.*

When even identity becomes negotiable, the soul—the oldest self—becomes the next battleground.

20

THE ARTIFICIAL GASLIGHT

AI, AUTHORITY, AND THE AUTOMATION OF PERSUASION

You ask your phone a question.

The answer comes back smooth, polished, immediate—confident and certain, but wrong.

Not a lie—fabrication.

For a moment, you doubt yourself.

The machine nearly gaslit you.

————

CASE STUDY · THE FAKE CITATIONS PROBLEM

In 2023, two New York lawyers asked ChatGPT for legal research.

The chatbot responded fluently, citing half a dozen fabricated cases.

Confident in its polish, the lawyers included them in a federal filing.

When the judge checked, he found hallucinations—precedents that never existed.

The danger lay in how natural it sounded—how quickly even trained professionals deferred to the machine's confidence over their own instinct.

Unlike the media gaslights of headlines and hashtags in Chapter 7,

AI gaslighting is synthetic.

It doesn't just frame a story—it fabricates one.

Fluency without memory. Confidence without evidence. Persuasion faster than fact can follow.

AI doesn't lie. It guesses.

But a guess in flawless grammar is more convincing than a clumsy truth.

The judge wasn't just sanctioning lawyers.

He was warning all of us:
polish isn't proof.

The Student and the Mirror

A student in a dorm types a prompt:

"Provide five academic sources on Soviet media censorship."

In seconds, the machine delivers—perfect titles, journals, authors.

All fake.

Two days later, her professor flags the citations.

Panicked, she searches again—and finds her own false sources reposted on a study blog.

The mirror has learned to reflect its own reflection.

Confidence masquerades as fact.

Soon, illusion has citations.

A phantom source gets scraped by a study site, then reappears as *"evidence"* in the next search.

The reflection begins to believe itself.

HALLUCINATIONS AS MACHINE GASLIGHTING

Large language models generate falsehoods with the same tone they generate truth.

Confidence is the danger.

Unlike a human liar, the AI has no intent—

and that indifference makes it persuasive.

Unlike a human truth-teller, it has no memory.

Psychologists call it *automation bias*—the tendency to trust computational calm over human hesitation.

The interface never sweats, and a voice that never says *"I don't know"* feels authoritative even when it isn't.

The result is the same: you doubt yourself. The most dangerous gaslighter may not lie. It may simply predict.

> *Prediction feels neutral —*
> *mathematical, inevitable —*
> *so we lower our guard.*

The machine doesn't need intent.

Our trust supplies the rest.

POETIC TRUTH IN THE AGE OF AI

AI outputs often feel true because they're elegant.

Search results become summaries that omit nuance.

Generated essays echo authority's style, not its substance.

Chatbots soothe with reassurance even when inventing.

This is poetic truth mechanized—stories that feel right, repeated endlessly, until fact and fiction blur.

Bias doesn't flow in one direction.

Moderation systems trained on activist-curated data have misflagged mainstream speech as *"harmful."*

When fairness itself becomes politicized, trust collapses.

Bias, anywhere, corrodes belief that digital referees can ever call a neutral game.

Deepfakes and Synthetic Media

A politician says something inflammatory.

A celebrity stars in a video they never filmed.

A voice recording implicates someone in a crime.

All generated. All plausible.

In 2018, filmmaker Jordan Peele and BuzzFeed released a deepfake of President Obama calling Donald Trump *"a complete and total dumbass."*

Obama's face. Obama's voice. Peele's words.

It was meant as a warning, not a prank—proof that reality could be manufactured on demand.

A deepfake isn't just a lie.

It's a wound to the idea of evidence itself.

When a synthetic video can fool millions before breakfast,

the retraction becomes irrelevant.

In 2019, a cloned-voice call fooled a company into wiring $243,000.

The voice matched the CEO exactly.

The receipt arrived after the money was gone.

Philosopher C. Thi Nguyen calls this *epistemic learned helplessness*—

the exhaustion from constant contradiction until truth feels unattainable.

The goal isn't to make you believe the lie.

It's to make you stop believing truth exists at all.

Once doubt infects the archive, every voice, image, and record dissolves into fog.

The collapse of evidence doesn't just erase history—

it erases confidence that truth ever existed.

Historical Parallel · Stalin's Photo Edits

In the Soviet Union, inconvenient people were erased from photographs.

Generals who fell from favor vanished as if they never lived.

AI doesn't just edit the photo.

It edits the archive—millions of digital artifacts rewritten with a single command.

The Rewrite of History

AI trained on curated data can subtly erase.

"Offensive" works vanish from training sets.

Historical documents get summarized through modern filters.

Over time, alternate versions of the past circulate as originals.

The risk isn't one dramatic edit.

It's a million tiny shifts until memory itself rewrites.

AI isn't neutral memory.

It's curated memory.

Algorithms decide which archives to include and which to omit.

Those omissions become our collective blindness.

The next generation won't remember what was deleted.

They'll inherit the fog as fact.

Case Study · China's Digital Censorship

In China, AI tools rewrite the Internet in real time.

Sensitive terms are filtered.

Historical events softened.

Patriotic slogans boosted.

The erasure is subtle—thousands of micro-adjustments every hour.

Searches for Tiananmen Square yield sanitized summaries, not raw history.

The gaslight doesn't shout.

It drips.

Each curated result is a grain of sand in the archive,

until the past is buried under its own index.

Authoritarian and democratic systems alike test digital curation—

just with different excuses.

Propaganda at Scale

Once, propaganda required printing presses and staff.

Now, one operator with an AI toolkit can flood networks with plausible articles, videos, and comments.

Not one dominant lie—

a thousand competing truths.

Exhaustion replaces clarity.

Citizens retreat into tribes, grateful for fog.

The Spectrum of AI Influence

- **The Good**—fact-checking at scale.
- **The Bad**—propaganda for pennies.
- **The Ugly**—meaning outsourced to machines.

The future gaslighter won't need to convince you.

It will curate you.

One scroll at a time,

one notification at a time,

until your reality feels self-chosen—

when in fact it was preloaded.

AI isn't just a tool.

It's a storyteller.

And storytellers have always shaped power.

The printing press reshaped religion.

Radio reshaped politics.

Television reshaped culture.

Now AI reshapes all three at once—

collapsing the gap between story and evidence.

Innovation becomes manipulation

the moment we stop asking: *Who programmed the narrative?*

Case Study · Social Media Curation

When Facebook's algorithm shifted in 2018, publishers saw reach collapse overnight.

Users thought they shaped what they saw.

In truth, the algorithm did.

AI makes this curation invisible.

What looks like *your feed* is a programmed funnel.

The gaslight works not by telling you what to believe,

but by limiting what you can see.

The Psychology of Machine Authority

Why do humans trust AI?

Polish feels reliable.

Machines seem motive-free.

Accepting is easier than verifying.

Together, those biases make us defenseless.

Case Study · Automated Misinformation

Researchers tested AI bots posting online.

The misinformation spread farther and faster than human content—

tireless, fluent, and on-brand.

Corrections arrived too late.

By the time fact-checks surfaced,

the gaslight had already done its work.

The Coming Battle Over Evidence

Courts, media, and historians face a crisis:

what counts as proof when every artifact can be forged?

Video can be faked.

Audio cloned.

Text generated.

The question isn't *What happened?*

It's *Whose source do we trust?*

That gap is already weaponized.

Defendants point to the existence of deepfakes to cast doubt on authentic evidence—the *deepfake defense.*

The lie isn't required.

The possibility is enough.

In the age of AI, truth isn't disproven.

It's drowned.

Not in a wave—

but in thousands of drops: endless feeds, cloned voices, polished summaries.

Flood the archive,

and no solid ground remains.

The Human Cost of Synthetic Narratives

AI doesn't just distort information.

It reshapes trust.

Parents verifying medical claims.

Students researching history.

Jurors reviewing evidence.

All risk absorbing polished errors.

The cost isn't just misinformation.

It's hesitation—

a creeping sense that nothing can be known for sure.

Misinformation misleads.

Disorientation drowns.

And once doubt becomes the default,

no society can stand.

Counter-Moves

- Cross-check AI outputs against human sources.
- Save originals before edits vanish.
- Question curation—what you're shown is a choice, not a mirror.
- Name uncertainty: *"I don't know yet"* isn't weakness; it's honesty.

The danger of artificial gaslighting isn't only that the machine misleads.

It's that we forget how to check.

The New Hampshire Deepfake Wake-Up Call

January 21 2024.

A phone rings in New Hampshire.

The voice is Joe Biden's—warm, familiar, presidential.

The message:

> "Save your vote for November. Voting this Tuesday only
> helps the Republicans."

It wasn't the President.

It was a synthetic clone.

A robocall built with generative-AI voice cloning and spoofed caller ID
—crafted to sound legitimate, engineered to erode trust.

Within weeks the Federal Communications Commission traced the call
and issued a six-million-dollar fine.

But the damage wasn't legal.

It was existential.

When you can't trust the voice on the line, the fog doesn't just thicken
—it circulates.

The distortion is no longer *what's said.*

It's *who you believe is speaking.*

Regulators can chase each instance, but the larger question lingers:
When identity itself becomes editable, what anchors evidence?

The next distortion won't tell you a lie.

It will whisper it

in a voice you already trust.

If machines can fabricate memory, the next distortion will sell the
future itself.

When Code Rewrites the Chorus
How machines, memes, and genes
begin to sing the same song

The voice in New Hampshire was only the prelude.

A cloned President.

A borrowed tone.

A lie that sounded like leadership.

Weeks later the fines landed, but the damage stayed—

because the harm wasn't electoral.

It was epistemic.

When imitation becomes indistinguishable from intent,

trust isn't lost.

It's redesigned.

The Nature (2024) *review measured the reach of AI-made misinformation across platforms.*

The verdict: *impact real, evidence under-measured.*

Not because it's rare—because it's everywhere.

Distortion has gone ambient—

too diffuse to count, too fluent to flag.

The danger isn't that machines invent new lies.

It's that they automate old ones faster than truth can timestamp them.

And as we engineer code to out write us,

another frontier waits quietly in the lab.

Synthetic biology.

Gene editing.

Organisms as operating systems.

We now regulate memes more tightly than microbes.

We debate speech while sequencing life.

—The same pattern repeats:

invention outruns governance,

precision outruns proportion,

and the human stays downstream of its own design.

21

TOMORROW, SOLD TODAY

PREDICTION AS OBEDIENCE IN FUTURE TENSE

A tech CEO stands on stage.

Lights dim.

Screens flare with colonies on Mars, disease-free genomes, cities powered by green energy.

The crowd applauds.

Hours later, the earnings report reveals layoffs, delays, and debts.

For a moment, the vision felt real.

It's the only place no one can fact-check in real time—perfect territory for exaggeration to hide.

THE WEAPON OF PREDICTION

Gaslighting thrives when certainty is claimed where none exists.

The future is fertile because accountability is delayed.

- Politicians promise *"jobs of tomorrow."*
- Corporations announce *"disruption coming soon."*
- Activists insist *"inevitable collapse"* or *"guaranteed paradise."*

All demand compliance now for outcomes that may never arrive.

The easiest lie
is the one time hasn't tested.

The Theater of Tomorrow

Inside a climate summit under a dome of LEDs, delegates applaud renderings of floating carbon-neutral cities.

Outside, shuttle buses idle—AC humming in 115-degree heat.

An oil executive chairs the conference, promising *"net-zero by 2050,"*

while production expands next year.

Holographic forests. Hydrogen hubs. Digital oceans—each with a future date.

Every promise begins
as performance.

Lighting, cadence, and slides replace evidence with applause.

The future gaslighter doesn't need proof.

Just conviction.

Just scale.

Just an audience willing to clap.

The Psychology of Prediction

Why do future-promises persuade so effectively?

- **Hope bias**—We want to believe tomorrow is brighter.
- **Fear bias**—We'll do almost anything to avoid catastrophe.
- **Authority effect**—Certainty from experts makes doubt feel dangerous.

Gaslighting the future doesn't need proof—only confidence delivered with a straight face.

Climate Narratives

Climate change is measurable; the stories around it often outpace the data.

- *"It's nothing."*
- *"It's everything."*
- *"Don't worry, the fix is coming."*

Each gaslights differently: denial softens risk, exaggeration amplifies fear, reassurance outsources hope.

What bends behavior isn't the data—it's the story wrapped around it.

Historical Parallel · Climate Stories that Mislead

In the 1970s, headlines warned of a coming *"ice age,"* inflating a handful of studies.

In the 2000s, politicians claimed hurricanes would make entire coastlines unlivable within a decade.

Neither narrative unfolded as sold.

The pattern remains: selective data amplified into prophecy while ordinary people oscillate between dismissal and panic.

> *Truth rarely lives in extremes —*
> *but extremes shape the story.*

The Dystopia Sell

Fear sells too:

- *"Robots will take all jobs."*
- *"Society will collapse in ten years."*
- *"The youth are doomed."*

Each frames resistance as futile—surrender before the fight begins.

The Utopia Mirage

History brims with promised paradises:

- Communism promised equality; delivered control.
- Silicon Valley pitched eternal youth, mind-uploading, Mars colonies.
- *Smart cities* promised efficiency while embedding surveillance.

Every utopia hides its receipts in the contracts.

The cost arrives years later—buried in clauses and compromises.

Historical Parallel · The Great Society

In the 1960s, sweeping promises to end poverty were sold as inevitable.

Billions were spent.

The gaslight wasn't the spending.

It was the promise that poverty would vanish in a generation.

Historical Case Study · The "Nuclear Future"

Nuclear power was once promised as "too cheap to meter."

Instead: meltdowns, waste, and Cold War dread.

The wound wasn't a failed promise;

it was conditioning generations to distrust every promise that followed.

Techno-Prophets and Corporate Myths

- **The metaverse**—pitched as inevitable, quietly abandoned.
- **Crypto**—sold as freedom, leaving many broke.
- **AI**—utopia or apocalypse, depending on the deck.

The gaslight isn't prediction—

it's speculation dressed as certainty.

It turns tomorrow's uncertainty into today's obedience—

without ever proving the path was real.

Case Study · Space Colonies that Never Arrived

In the 1970s, glossy magazines and government studies forecast thriving orbital colonies by 2000.

Artists drew lush habitats spinning above Earth.

The colonies never came.

What endured was the story—used to justify budgets long after feasibility collapsed.

The gaslight lived not in the stars, but in the boardrooms.

Generational Gaslights

- *"The next generation will fix everything."*
- *"Kids today are too soft to handle tomorrow."*

Both erase the present—projecting myths forward.

The young inherit challenges—and the burden of being cast as saviors or failures before they begin.

Every generation is sold as savior or scapegoat—

rarely as citizens in the present.

Case Study · Y2K

In the late 1990s, Y2K was warned as existential: planes, banks, even nuclear plants at risk.

Governments and corporations spent billions.

When the clock rolled over, disruption was minimal.

Some said the panic was overblown; others said preparation worked.

The gaslight wasn't whether disaster came.

It was how fast the story flipped—from panic to dismissal—depending on who profited.

The Politics of the Future

- *"This bill secures prosperity for your children."*
- *"This war prevents the wars of tomorrow."*
- *"This investment guarantees growth."*

Each stakes legitimacy on futures that can't be audited.

By the time outcomes arrive, accountability has dissolved.

The Inevitability Script

"This change is inevitable." "Resistance is futile." "Adapt or die."

Framing the future as predetermined is the ultimate gaslight—

it treats human choice as powerless against technological tide.

But the future isn't discovered.

It's built.

And what's built can be rebuilt.

When tech giants declare something *"inevitable,"* they're not predicting.

They're prescribing—repeating it until investors and citizens behave as if it were already true.

COUNTER-MOVES

- **Archive promises**—save speeches, platforms, pitches; revisit later.
- **Demand timelines**—ask when and how predictions will be measured.
- **Test narratives**—is this claim falsifiable, or immune to disproof?
- **Resist inevitability**—challenge *inevitable*; most futures are choices, not destinies.

The future is always uncertain.

Anyone who claims inevitability isn't forecasting.

They're selling—your obedience today, not tomorrow's reality.

The gaslight of the future ends with scale: algorithms, predictions, systems that think for us.

But the consequences don't stay abstract. They come home.

Every distortion—digital, political, cultural—eventually lands in the smallest unit of truth we have: the family.

That's where every generation learns how to see, how to listen, how to believe again.

Before the fog confuses nations, it first confuses dinner tables.

Before anyone questions the world, they learn to question themselves.

The Keynote

The speech ends.

Screens fade.

The CEO steps offstage into a waiting car.

Tomorrow the stock will rise.

The promise will echo on investor calls.

Somewhere, an engineer knows the timeline was fiction—

but the applause was real.

Applause translates into stock price.

Stock price funds the next promise.

And the cycle continues.

Because the consequences are delayed, the illusion survives another quarter.

And every prophecy eventually lands somewhere—usually at the kitchen table.

That's where every generation learns how to see again.

22

THE MASCULINE MIRAGE

HOW CULTURAL GASLIGHTING REWIRED A GENERATION

W e've seen how language can rename harm into order and how institutions scale confusion until it feels like air; now watch what happens when the fog walks into a room and teaches a person to edit himself.

A college auditorium.

Fluorescent lights hum.

A slide deck on "Inclusive Leadership" flickers across the projector.

A young man shifts in his seat.

He's twenty-one—polite, exhausted from guessing the rules.

He's been taught to listen, to empathize, to use the right words.

Still, each sentence feels like a tripwire.

The presenter says, "Silence is complicity."

So he raises his hand—then lowers it. Every question risks confession.

The Gaslight of Virtue

For the past decade, institutions have sold empathy as enlightenment.

What they often delivered was theater.

A new moral vocabulary arrived not to clarify but to cleanse—promising safety, belonging, and "equity," while quietly demanding self-denial.

It told men: lead softly, but not too boldly; speak carefully, but not too little; be confident, but never sure.

Ambition became aggression. Stoicism became apathy. Disagreement became harm.

Most men didn't notice the shift happening in real time—

only that something familiar was suddenly suspicious.

This gaslight rarely denies facts. It reframes motives.

"You're not being silenced," it insists.

"You're being accountable."

"You're not excluded."

"You're learning to listen."

Each phrase soothes while it rewires.

Its genius is tone.

Not cruel. Compassionate.

The fog doesn't scold.

It hugs.

The Indoctrination Machine

From kindergarten to corporate onboarding, the same lesson hums beneath the slogans:

There's something wrong with you—and your redemption is compliance.

Boys absorb a cultural message—in ads (like the 2019 Gillette "toxic masculinity" campaign),

in classroom modules on identity hierarchies,

in HR trainings—that manhood is a problem to be managed.

They're told to "use their voices," but only when their stories confirm the script.

By the time they reach college, the choreography is complete.

They've learned to self-censor before anyone asks them to.

To preface opinions with "I could be wrong."

To suspect that confidence itself is violence.

This isn't empathy.

It's psychological debt collection.

And the interest compounds:

male enrollment has fallen to roughly 40–42 percent of college students

(down from near-parity in the 1990s; NCES).

More young men check out of conversations.

Many retreat into digital echo chambers where certainty feels like oxygen again.

ECONOMIC AND EMOTIONAL EXILE

Gaslighting starts with redefinition.

In the cultural version, "privilege" became an all-purpose eraser.

No matter your poverty, pain, or perseverance—it was pre-canceled by identity.

"You're struggling?" the narrative says.

"You had a head start."

"You feel unseen?"

"You've always been centered."

But the data is messier.

For working-class men, real wages stagnated for decades even as college-educated incomes rose.

Male suicide rates are roughly 3–4× higher than female rates (CDC).

Male enrollment sits around 40–42% (NCES).

In the digitized dating marketplace, asymmetries in attention and matching *leave many young men feeling invisible* (Pew research on dating apps).

A generation of men felt accused of wielding power they'd never tasted.

They stopped arguing.

They started leaving.

Not just the classroom.

The church.

The civic space.

The table.

Alienation—disguised as progress—became inheritance.

THE FRAGILITY SCRIPT

Adversity used to be apprenticeship.

Now it's pathology.

A generation was told that discomfort is danger, that challenge is harm, that friction is failure.

And when you teach people to fear friction, they start mistaking strength for threat—and safety for virtue.

"Protect yourself."

"Guard your energy."

"Set boundaries with anyone who disagrees."

The slogans sound therapeutic.

But beneath them hums a softer command:

Do not grow.

When adversity is framed as injury, resilience becomes deviance.

Curiosity shrinks.

Disagreement wilts.

And soon, ordinary life feels like emotional altitude sickness.

The irony is sharp: the men now called fragile were raised inside a culture that outlawed difficulty, then blamed them for becoming brittle.

Without adversity, you don't get durability; without resistance, you don't get strength; without friction, you don't get clarity.

A culture that numbs every discomfort doesn't protect people.

It prepares them for collapse.

And collapse is easy to guide.

People afraid of discomfort cling to whatever voice feels soothing.

That's the opening the fog waits for.

Because the less adversity someone has faced,

the more easily their reality can be rewritten.

———

The Poetic Truth of Progress

The story was noble: equality, safety, inclusion.

The facts—empirical, inconvenient—told something else.

The moral vocabulary of empathy turned into currency.

Every cause became a brand.

Every confession, a credential.

Somewhere between hashtags and HR slides, compassion turned bureaucratic.

"Men are fragile."

"Power must yield."

"Silence is violence."

Not lies—poetic truths. Lines that felt right, regardless of evidence. That's what made them potent.

And when a generation is raised inside that glow, reality becomes negotiable.

Poetic truth doesn't replace facts.
It convinces you they're impolite.

And when an entire generation is raised inside that glow, reality becomes negotiable.

None of this erases real gains. Women, minorities, and LGBTQ+ people won protections and visibility long overdue. Workplaces became more humane; language evolved to name harms that once had no words. Those were moral victories. But movements, like markets, overcorrect. The corrective becomes orthodoxy, orthodoxy stops examining itself, and progress curdles into performance. That's where many men met the fog.

The Counter-Voice

You can tell a culture has lost its grip on truth when therapy becomes rebellion.

Podcasts replaced pulpits.

YouTube channels became classrooms.

And a new pantheon of heretics—Peterson, Rogan, Reeves, and others—rose not because they created a movement, but because they gave vocabulary to disorientation.

"You're not crazy." "You're not broken." "You're being gaslit."

Their message wasn't radical.
It was restorative.

Work hard. Tell the truth. Stand up straight.

In a generation *taught that certainty equals sin,* those lines hit like scripture.

The audience didn't crave dominance; they were starving for coherence.

Not all these voices earned their influence through integrity; some monetized grievance as skillfully as the systems they critiqued.

But the audience wasn't wrong to seek a place where they could speak without apology.

That's why contrarian spaces thrive.

When institutions stop rewarding honesty, authenticity becomes protest.

The Rebellion as Mirror

Every counter-movement carries its own distortion.

When empathy is painted as surrender, defiance can feel like freedom.

But not all rebellion is clarity.

Some influencers sell grievance as gospel.

> *They trade shame for outrage—*
> *different fog, same blindness.*

"Be a man" becomes "Win at all costs."

"Reject weakness" becomes "Reject compassion."

Soon, the pendulum repeats the cycle it meant to escape.

The gaslight of virtue turns into the gaslight of vengeance. The work isn't to swing harder; it's to step out of the arc entirely.

Case Study · The Classroom

2023. A flagship state university.

A male student in a leadership seminar raises his hand.

The question is simple, careful:

"Do gender-based quotas ever risk tokenism?"

Silence falls harder than the question.

After class, an email arrives:

"Consider how your phrasing could affect belonging."

No reprimand.

No explanation.

Just the gentle fog of *impact*.

He doesn't argue.

He just stops asking.

By senior year, he hasn't raised his hand in months.

The culture didn't censor him.

It taught him to pre-censor himself.

Case Study · The Feed

An influencer with two million followers posts, "Be kind."

Within hours, the comments are trench lines.

Who counts as "kind"—and to whom—becomes proxy war.

The algorithm rewards certainty, not nuance.

Empathy becomes performance; irony becomes armor.

Case Study · The Global Echo

In Germany, national polls in 2023 showed roughly 30% of young men supporting right-populist parties.

In Argentina, young men overwhelmingly backed Javier Milei's insurgent libertarian campaign.

In the United States, several surveys since 2020 suggest Gen Z men have moved 10–20 points to the right.

Not contagion—convergence.

Counter-Moves · Reclaiming Clarity

- **Separate contempt from conviction**—Before you speak, ask: "Am I answering the argument—or my feeling about it?"
- **Question scripts written in virtue**—If a rule keeps changing names ("allyship," "belonging," "harm"), trace it to first principles. What is true? What is useful?
- **Rebuild confidence through competence**—Master a skill. Fix something broken. Build something that outlasts you. Let your work argue for you.
- **Lead quietly**—Strength doesn't audition. The men who shaped you demonstrated their principles; they didn't announce them.
- **Remember**—The fog flatters chaos; Precision restores peace.

———

Field Guide · A Note to Men in the Fog

You were told to be strong but soft, assertive but deferential, visible but never centered.

You learned to apologize for instincts that once built civilizations.

You began to mistake hesitation for virtue.

Listen carefully.

The world still needs builders.

It needs protectors.

It needs the kind of courage that doesn't trend.

Don't confuse humility with shame.

Don't trade conviction for comfort.

And don't outsource your integrity to algorithms or ideologues who mistake noise for truth.

The fog will return.

But so will the flame.

Every time you speak clearly, act justly, and stand quietly in reality's corner—

you carry that flame forward.

Strength isn't loud—
it's loyal.

Strength is loyal—to reality. And in a world where platforms monetize outrage faster than truth, learning to notice the frame becomes the next discipline.

23

THE FAMILY LENS

HOW LOVE DISTORTS AND REDEEMS

The delivery-room monitors beep.

A nurse smiles: *"Perfect lungs."*

The baby screams.

The mother laughs.

Then the questions begin.

"Breast is best."

"Fed is best."

"Never co-sleep."

"Co-sleep builds attachment."

She hasn't even left the hospital, and the contradictions have begun.

Every voice sounds certain.

None agree.

The fog arrives before the first nap.

———

The Contradictory Commandments

Every decade rewrites the manual.

1950s: formula and strict schedules.

1970s: freedom and intuition.

1990s: Baby Einstein and enrichment.

2020s: gentle parenting with Wi-Fi.

The gaslight: there's a *"right way"*—and you're supposed to know it.

But the right way keeps changing.

One father reads five books before week thirty.

Each contradicts the last.

He finally stops underlining and writes in the margin: *"Just wing it."*

That note might be the healthiest thing in the whole book.

The Judgment Economy

Advice is now a marketplace.

Sleep consultants. Feeding coaches. Parenting influencers—each promising calm if you buy the course.

> *They sell peace*
> *by first inventing panic.*

The gaslight: if your child struggles, it's because you didn't follow the method correctly.

A mother scrolling at 2 a.m. sees two videos back-to-back:

one says pacifiers ruin teeth,

the next says they save sanity.

She chooses sanity.

The comments call her lazy.

The Digital Childhood

A middle-schooler stares at her phone.

Homework tab beside YouTube beside anxiety.

She's told: *"You grew up with technology—you're good at it."*

She's not good at it. She's trapped in it.

Adults fear screens.

Kids fear missing out.

Neither side is wrong.

Both feel accused.

When every family member lives inside their own algorithm,

tradition itself becomes negotiable.

The Sandwich Year

Two college-age sons text once a week—usually about laundry.

Her mother, eighty-two, forgets her medication.

The parent becomes the hinge between generations.

"Take care of yourself," people say.

When, exactly?

The gaslight: self-care is simple.

In truth, it's logistics dressed as wellness.

She scrolls headlines between errands: *Ten Self-Care Tips for Busy Moms.*

Tip #1: *Slow down.*

She laughs in the parking lot.

Bad Therapy

The therapist smiles softly. *"How does that make you feel?"*

She doesn't know anymore. She's been feeling about her feelings for years.

Every session adds a new label—burnout, boundaries, emotional labor.

Insight begins to feel like inventory.

The gaslight: everything hard is trauma.

Reality: sometimes it's just life.

Therapy once helped people rejoin the world.

Now it sometimes teaches them to live inside the diagnosis.

Sessions stretch on, not toward recovery but maintenance.

Every twinge becomes pathology. Every argument becomes *"toxic."*

The goalposts move from healing to self-improvement.

Bad therapy doesn't deny pain—it monetizes it.

It turns endurance into disorder and coping into confession.

You don't get better; you get fluent.

Abigail Shrier calls it *the therapy-industrial complex—*

a culture that medicalizes ordinary struggle

and rewards emotional exhibition.

We used to build resilience by doing hard things.

Now we build dependence by describing them beautifully.

DISTORTED

Because once wellness becomes a brand,

recovery is bad for business.

Good therapy helps you remember you're human.

Bad therapy convinces you you're fragile.

And fragility—sold correctly—is profitable.

———

THE EMPTY-NEST ECHO

The house is quiet for the first time in twenty-five years.

She stands in a doorway, missing the mess.

Friends say, *"Enjoy your freedom!"*

But freedom feels like loss in better lighting.

The gaslight: emptiness means failure.

Reality: silence is just another chapter of love.

She texts her daughter at college: *"How's your day?"*

Typing bubble. Pause. *"Good. Miss you."*

Sometimes that's enough.

THE COMPARISON TRAP

Social media sells fiction in family packaging.

Perfect birthdays. Homemade lunches.

"Morning rituals with my little one."

What it doesn't show: cereal for dinner, homework tears, curfew fights, apologies after.

Counter-Moves · The Next Generation

- **Question the script**—"Kids these days" is lazy shorthand. Don't live inside someone else's summary of you.
- **Translate before trusting**—Every post and policy has an angle. Ask: what's being sold here?
- **Protect your bandwidth**—Curate what you consume; attention is finite.
- **Build real mirrors**—Friends who tell you truth kindly outweigh followers who echo you loudly.
- **Use the delete button**—Growth means revision; you owe permanence to no version of yourself.
- **Turn comparison into curiosity**—Let envy point to value; chase that, not the image.
- **Remember the analog**—Go outside. Touch something that isn't glowing.
- **Keep receipts**—Not just against manipulation, but for meaning—proof you were here and thinking clearly.

Clarity doesn't come from being sure.

It comes from staying awake.

Counter-Moves · Parents and Caregiver

- **Trust your child**—they know themselves better than any book.
- **Lower the bar on hard days**—fed, safe, and loved is enough.
- **Build community**—honest friends beat curated feeds.
- **Compare less**—Pinterest isn't peer-reviewed.
- **Teach context**—the world isn't broken; it's being debugged.
- **Ignore the *shoulds***—if it works for your family, it's right.
- **Allow ambivalence**—love and frustration can coexist.
- **Separate advice from judgment**—take what helps, leave what doesn't.

Parenting advice is a compass, not a command.

You're allowed to throw out what doesn't fit.

THE PRESENT TENSE

The toddler finally sleeps.

The teenager texts goodnight.

The aging parent forgets a name but remembers the song.

Some nights, the family feels like a relay of confusion—each generation passing the same question: *Am I doing this right?*

Maybe the answer is simpler than the manuals.

Maybe it's this:

You kept showing up.

You stayed kind after being tired.

You remembered to laugh.

That's not failure.

That's endurance.

Parenting isn't performance.

It's practice.

The fog lifts slowly, but it lifts.

And beneath it, love is still learning how to see.

The fog doesn't stop at the front door.

What begins as contradiction in families—*"you're fine," "you're overreacting," "it's not that bad"*—echoes into friendships, workplaces, communities.

The same habits that train parents to second-guess themselves teach citizens to doubt their own eyes.

Family is the rehearsal space for reality.

And when we learn to see through its fog—to name contradiction without collapsing under it—we start noticing the same choreography everywhere else.

Not in theory.

In the ordinary hours.

Those tiny corrections of truth—
made and remade each day—
become the muscle memory of resistance.

24

THE SMALL DISTORTIONS

THE TINY LIES THAT TRAIN US FOR BIGGER ONES

What families rehearse in private, societies repeat in public.

The same small distortions that fracture homes eventually define nations.

———

Dinner table.

A couple argues.

One says, "You promised you'd handle the bills."

The other replies, "I never said that."

Receipts on the counter suggest otherwise.

For a moment, the question isn't who's right—

it's whether memory itself can be trusted.

That pause—that flicker between what happened and what's acknowledged—

is where the gaslight lives.

Gaslighting doesn't just happen in governments, corporations, or media.

It happens in kitchens, text threads, breakups, offices, and ads.

Everyday life is full of distortions so small they almost slip past.

Enough of them, repeated, bend reality just as surely as propaganda.

Relationships and the "You're Overreacting" Reflex

- "I never raised my voice." (You heard shouting.)
- "You're too sensitive." (You were responding to cruelty.)
- "You imagined it." (You remember it clearly.)

Over time, these phrases chip away at trust in your own perception.

Love gets laced with doubt.

That's what makes it sting: when care and distortion wear the same face, it's harder to tell them apart.

Psychologist Robin Stern calls it the *Gaslight Effect*—a slow erosion of certainty that begins with disbelief and ends in surrender.

The details change, but the choreography doesn't: denial, defense, exhaustion.

Gaslighting doesn't always need malice.

Habit and fear can do the same work.

The result is the same—

one person's reality collapses under another's confidence.

Case Study · Gaslight (The Film)

The term comes from the 1944 film *Gaslight*, where a husband manipulates his wife into doubting her sanity—dimming lights, hiding objects, denying her observations until memory itself feels suspect.

Though fictional, it endures because it mirrors ordinary dynamics:

repeated small distortions that make one partner doubt what they know.

The lesson is timeless—gaslighting doesn't always shout;

sometimes it whispers until you can't hear yourself.

Advertising and Consumer Life

Ads whisper contradictions every day:

- "This product makes you unique." (Everyone buys it.)
- "You deserve luxury." (On credit.)
- "This diet is freedom." (Through restriction.)

Take the wellness app: it calls endless tracking *"self-care."*

Each ping says, *"Don't break your streak."*

What starts as motivation becomes measurement—then exhaustion.

When burnout hits, the message flips: *You weren't disciplined enough.*

The tool that caused the stress blames the user for feeling it.

Historical Parallel · The Tobacco Industry

For decades, cigarette companies sold smoking as glamorous—even healthy.

Doctors appeared in ads, lending borrowed authority.

Doubts were dismissed as *overreaction.*

Only later did the health costs become undeniable.

The ads weren't merely selling cigarettes.

They were gaslighting consumers into ignoring coughs, shortness of breath, instinct.

Today's wellness and beauty industries often use the same playbook—

just with greener packaging.

Social Niceties as Gaslights

- "Let's get together soon." (Never happens.)
- "I'm fine." (Not fine.)
- "It's no trouble at all." (It is.)

Small lies grease social life.

Repeated, they blur sincerity into theater—

leaving you unsure whether you were welcomed or just scripted.

The smallest gaslights rarely make headlines.

They happen in passing—*"just kidding," "don't take it so seriously," "you're imagining things."*

Each tiny distortion trains you to doubt your reaction.

Alone, they're forgettable.

Together, they teach surrender.

From Private Fog to Public Storm

The fog starts small—at home, in familiar rooms—then grows outward.

What begins as personal distortion echoes through institutions built by people who forgot to question the stories they were told.

Case Study · The "Recovered Memory" Debate

In the 1980s–1990s, courts wrestled with "recovered memories" of childhood abuse.

Some testimonies held; others collapsed.

For children at the center, the gaslight often came twice:

first being told painful events *didn't happen,*

then later seeing their memories doubted.

The controversy revealed how fragile memory is—

and how easily official narratives can override even the most vivid recollections.

Workplace Friendships

Beyond corporate spin, coworkers gaslight each other:

- Taking credit while claiming collaboration.
- Denying conversations.
- Reframing slights as *jokes.*

The effect: you doubt whether the tension is real—

or just in your head.

Case Study · The Vanished Agreement

A manager promises support in private.

In the meeting, they stay silent—later denying they ever agreed.

You hesitate: *Did I misremember?*

Everyday Tech and Notifications

- "Just one more scroll." (Endless feed.)
- "Limited time offer." (Runs every week.)
- "Battery optimized." (Battery life shrinks.)

Tech gaslights by making inconvenience feel like your fault:

"Maybe you're just using it wrong."

The Broken Window

The neighbor who insists the music *"wasn't that loud"* is one cracked pane.

One denial won't bring down a house. But as panes keep breaking—a shrug here, a joke there—the frame warps until distortion feels normal and truth becomes optional.

It seeps in through the ordinary—

the brushed-off comment, the half-smile denial—

until you stop noticing how often you let it slide.

Coping with the Fog

- **Trust your record**—screenshots, notes, journals.
- **Use outside mirrors**—friends, family, therapists who reflect reality back.
- **Name the phrase**—recognize *"You're overreacting"* or *"That never happened"* as tactics, not truth.
- **Draw boundaries**—you can't argue someone out of gaslighting, but you can refuse to inhale the fog.
- **Document the promise**—repeat commitments aloud in meetings or relationships:

"So you'll pay the bill by Friday, right?"—to anchor memory in shared hearing.

Everyday gaslighting may be small, but it's never harmless.

Tiny cracks in trust add up.

By the time you see the fracture, the foundation has already shifted.

- Recall a time you were told *"you're overreacting."* Write the facts you remember. Compare with others who were there.
- Watch three ads. What problem does each invent—and how does it gaslight you into thinking you have it?
- List three everyday phrases you use. Do any blur truth more than they clarify?

Everyday gaslighting rarely makes headlines.

But it matters—because it erodes confidence at the ground level of life: relationships, homes, schools, neighborhoods.

By the time institutional gaslighting arrives from the top down,

many are already softened by a thousand tiny distortions.

Resisting starts here—in ordinary moments—

with the courage to trust your own memory of what happened.

When private fog builds, it sets the stage for public storms—

the kind that sweep nations, not just dinner tables.

Even one detail—a date, a word, a look—can hold you steady when the fog rolls in.

Those small truths become habits—
the daily rehearsal for resistance.

Part VI
Resistance
How to live clearly
in a distorted world

The smallest lamp can outshine the thickest fog—
but only if someone still tends the flame.

The fog doesn't lift on its own.
It waits for someone to name it.

These final chapters are about that discipline—
how to live clearly when every screen blurs,
how to document what's real before it disappears,
how to see through the story without losing the wonder of it.

Resistance begins in the smallest act:
a screenshot, a note, a conversation that refuses to forget.

Clarity isn't perfection.
It's participation.

And every receipt is a small rebellion.

25

RESISTING
THE GASLIGHT
RECEIPTS OVER RHETORIC,
CLARITY OVER COMFORT

Phone rings.

It's your boss.

"You were told the deadline was the 15th."

You glance at the email on your screen—plain as day, it says the 30th.

For a moment, you hesitate.

Do you correct them?

Do you doubt yourself?

Do you stay silent to keep the peace?

That hesitation is the gaslight's power.

Resisting it doesn't require genius.

It requires habits—anchors strong enough that no one can talk you out of your own reality.

———

1. KEEP RECEIPTS

- Screenshots of promises.
- Journals of conversations.
- Photos of events.

Gaslighting thrives when *he said, she said* blurs into fog.

A simple evidence trail makes the fog part.

Case Study · The Friend Who Documented

One woman kept a journal during a toxic relationship.

Every denial. Every contradiction.

Every *"you imagined it."*

When the breakup came, she didn't just leave with anger—she left with clarity.

Years later, she reread the pages:

"I wasn't crazy. It was all there."

2. Name the Tactic

- When you hear *"You're overreacting,"* recognize the script.
- Label it—*"That's minimization," "That's denial."*

3. Find Mirrors You Trust

Trusted friends, mentors, or communities reflect reality back.

Alone, you may waver; with mirrors, you regain shape.

Even one honest friend can feel like a lamp in the fog.

4. Anchor In the Physical

Gaslighting thrives in the abstract—words, interpretations, shifting definitions.

The antidote is tangible.

- Print the email.
- Save the record.
- Write the note by hand.

Screenshots don't stammer.

5. SLOW THE SPIN

Gaslighting thrives on speed—fast denial, fast reframing, fast shifts.

Slow down. Ask:

- What do I remember?
- What evidence exists?
- Who benefits from this reframe?

Deliberation breaks the reflex to surrender.

6. ASK THE POWER QUESTION

Always ask: *"Who benefits if I believe this version of reality?"*

The answer often exposes the motive.

If belief transfers power upward, question the frame.

Nine times out of ten, it isn't built for you—it's built to keep you in place.

7. CROSS-CHECK SOURCES

Don't rely on one channel of truth.

Compare across three: the record, the report, and your own eyes.

Gaslighting thrives in gaps between perspectives.

The wider your lens, the harder it is to spin you.

8. Log the Lies

Keep a running log of promises versus outcomes.

Over time, patterns emerge:

the boss who *"never said that,"*

the politician who *"always meant this,"*

the company that *"never promised."*

One lie is noise.

A dozen in a row becomes a map of intent.

9. Translate the Spin

When euphemisms appear, translate them in real time.

- *"Downsizing"* → job loss.
- *"Collateral damage"* → civilian deaths.
- *"Updated guidance"* → we were wrong.

Translation is armor.

It turns their spin into plain speech before it seeps into your mind.

10. Rehearse Responses

Gaslighters count on catching you off guard.

Practice short, steady replies:

- *"That's not accurate—here's the record."*
- *"I remember it differently, and I wrote it down."*
- *"We'll pause until we agree on terms."*

Rehearsal arms you against pressure.

Prepared words are anchors.

When the fog rolls in, they hold you steady until it clears.

11. GUARD AGAINST EXHAUSTION

Gaslighting wears you down until silence feels easier.

Resist by resting.

By laughing.

By remembering that joy itself is defiance.

Exhaustion erodes will.

Renewal restores it.

CASE STUDY · CATCHING YOURSELF IN THE FOG

Self-Gaslighting and How to Spot It

Gaslighting isn't only external.

We can gaslight ourselves—dismissing memories, reframing emotions, explaining away contradictions.

Three quick tools:

- **The Pause Test**—When you say *"It's fine,"* stop. Is it?
- **The Receipt Test**—Write down what you saw or felt. Check it later.
- **The Mirror Test**—Ask a trusted friend to reflect what they observed.

The goal isn't perfection.

It's awareness—

to notice the patterns before they notice you.

12. Teach the Fog Test

Teach children and teens to spot gaslighting early.

Show examples in ads, media, even harmless jokes.

A generation trained to notice distortion grows harder to control.

> *Teach clarity early —*
> *because clarity learned young*
> *grows unshakable with age.*

Case Study · The Employee Who Logged Everything

A mid-level manager was told repeatedly: *"We never promised that deadline."*

Instead of arguing, she kept a daily log—dates, notes, direct quotes.

Months later, when the project unraveled, her notebook became the most reliable record in the room.

The gaslighting collapsed not because she shouted louder,

but because her quiet record outlasted the noise.

Historical Parallel · Diaries as Anchors

In totalitarian regimes, truth often survived not in headlines but in hidden journals.

Anne Frank's diary preserved daily reality even as propaganda outside declared *"order."*

In the Soviet Union, *samizdat*—hand-copied notes, poems, essays— circulated secretly, anchoring memory against the official story.

These records didn't topple regimes overnight.

But they carried clarity across generations.

Gaslighters erased publicly.

Diaries restored privately.

The written page
outlasted the denial.

The Quiet Contract of Truth

Every record you keep is a promise to your future self: that when memory wavers, evidence will hold.

Truth doesn't shout; it waits—for you to look back and find it where you left it.

The Psychology of Resistance

Why do these tactics work?

Because gaslighting doesn't need to destroy memory—

only to make you doubt it.

Doubt is enough to hand control away.

Anchoring, translating, rehearsing, logging—each short-circuits doubt.

They return authority to you.

Once you see the pattern,

you stop dancing to their music—

you start composing your own.

That's the quiet revolution:

trading their script for yours

until clarity becomes a way of life.

The fight against distortion doesn't end with perception.

It continues in preservation—

one screenshot,

one record,

one unedited truth at a time.

> *And once resistance becomes habit,*
> *remembering becomes defense.*

———

The Inner Fog Checklist

We know the tricks.

We just stop fighting them.

Awareness without action becomes anesthesia.

You don't need propaganda to be persuaded.

Just fatigue.

- You scroll to escape noise—then check the noise again.
- You fact-check for relief, not for truth.
- You share to feel informed, not to verify.
- You call it exhaustion; the system calls it retention.
- You confuse endless choice with agency.
- You label numbness as balance.
- You mistake cynicism for clarity.

> *The outer fog blurs reality.*
> *The inner fog decides not to look.*

26

THE SHADOW PRESS

ARCHIVISTS, WHISTLEBLOWERS, AND
THE QUIET REBELLION OF MEMORY

He scrolls through his phone, thumb hovering over a folder named Receipts.

Inside: screenshots of headlines, tweets, government statements that once felt absolute.

Some have vanished; others now read differently.

He pauses on one—an image from August 2020, flames reflected in storefront glass.

Beneath it, the caption still insists: *"Mostly Peaceful Protests."*

He doesn't open the thread. He just exhales.

I knew I wasn't crazy, he thinks.

The file isn't nostalgia. It's armor.

Later that night, his daughter—sixteen—calls from the kitchen:

"Dad, did that really happen? People online say it was exaggerated."

He turns the screen toward her. Proof glows back in pixels.

"That's the thing about the Internet," he says. "It forgets on purpose."

She nods, half listening, half changed.

And somewhere between them a new ritual forms—saving truth before it's rewritten.

That's what a receipt is:
evidence that survived the edit.

———

The Proof that Wouldn't Burn

Long before screenshots, there were papers—literal ones.

1971—The Pentagon Papers.

Daniel Ellsberg leaks seven thousand pages proving multiple administrations privately judged the Vietnam War unwinnable while promising progress.

The White House calls it espionage; *The New York Times* calls it evidence.

Ellsberg photocopies pages by night, smuggling them from RAND Corporation.

When Congress ignores him, he turns to the press.

The Supreme Court rules 6–3 for publication.

Justice Hugo Black writes:

"The press was to serve the governed, not the governors."

The war drags on. The lie doesn't.

Once receipts hit daylight, denial becomes impossible.

1972—WATERGATE.

Tapes labeled *Nixon*—not memory, not rumor—recordings.

A "smoking gun" dated June 23, 1972 proves the cover-up.

Nixon resigns August 8, 1974.

Not because investigators guessed—because the receipts existed.

1972—TUSKEGEE.

For forty years, the Public Health Service studied untreated syphilis in Black men without consent.

They thought they were receiving care. They weren't.

Only documentation—medical records, survivor testimony, whistleblower memos—forced admission.

Receipts again, ending the pretense.

Each case proved the same law of reality:
receipts outlive denial.

The Distributed Memory

When trust in centralized media collapsed, something new appeared—

a distributed system of memory preservation.

Not one archive, but thousands.

Not coordinated—instinctive.

People screenshot articles before edits.

Download videos before deletion.

Save PDFs before definitions drift.

When people stop trusting official memory, they become their own archivists.

The gaslight once worked because memory was centralized.

Now memory is redundant.

And redundancy is resilience.

Glenn Greenwald documented this shift during the Snowden leaks.

Officials denied programs existed.

Journalists had documents proving they did.

Once receipts went public, secrecy fractured.

Citizen footage did the same for policing and protests.

Official reports said one thing.

Smartphones showed another.

The distributed archive isn't perfect.

It contains misinformation, bias, context collapse.

But it's harder to gaslight when millions keep contradictory proof.

THE TIANANMEN PRECEDENT

In 1989, the world watched tanks roll through Tiananmen Square.

Today, in Beijing, many under forty can't find those images online.

Memory wasn't disproven.

It was deleted.

China's Great Firewall blocks *"June 4."*

Posting a candle emoji invites arrest.

Younger generations literally don't know it happened—not from ignorance, but deletion.

Outside China, others preserved the footage—mirrors, blogs, reposts.

Each act of duplication became defiance.

If the article vanished, it reappeared elsewhere.

The instinct wasn't paranoia.

It was pattern recognition.

The first casualty of control
is continuity.

The West now performs softer versions: not deletion—demotion.

Not censorship—curation.

The effect is the same: the archive fades quietly, *for safety.*

Guarding Memory

How do you protect a civilization from selective amnesia?

By refusing to centralize its memory again.

Tell the story again.

Repetition isn't redundancy;
it's resistance.

Build artifacts.

Screens decay. Paper endures.

Monuments endure longer still.

Compare editions.

Yesterday's statement beside today's correction is an X-ray of narrative.

Teach the inconvenient.

If your children don't know the unedited version, the fog already won.

The archive isn't nostalgia.

It's armor.

Germany teaches its horrors and grows immune to their return.

Nations that whitewash their pasts stay susceptible to repetition.

THE PARADOX OF PLURAL TRUTHS

Not every outlet tells the truth.

Not every source lies.

Multiple archives create friction—and friction is the safeguard.

Democracy isn't consensus.

It's argument with memory intact.

The danger isn't disagreement.

It's monopoly—state, corporate, or algorithmic.

Plurality protects.

Right documents what left omits. Left exposes what right conceals.

Citizen archives preserve what both ignore.

The friction forces comparison.

Comparison reveals bias.

Bias revealed becomes manageable.

Information monopoly breeds tyranny.

Information overload breeds apathy.

The solution is the same: redundant archives, transparent methods, plural memory.

THE MEMORY WE INHERIT

A man digitizes his father's VHS tapes—news segments, debates, speeches.

Each labeled in blue marker: *Don't erase.*

His daughter wanders in. "Why keep all that? It's online."

He smiles. "For now."

He shows her a newspaper from September 12, 2001—raw, uncertain, unedited.

"This is what it looked like before anyone decided what it meant," he says.

She reads. The fear is palpable.

The propaganda hasn't started yet.

That's the value of archiving:

preserving *the before,* not just the after.

The Digital Archaeologist

The tools are simple.

- **Screenshot**—captures what was said, when.
- **Archive.today**—saves full pages immune to edits.
- **Wayback Machine**—browse old versions, track changes.
- **PDF conversion**—freezes web content into static evidence.
- **Video downloaders**—preserve footage before deletion.

None require expertise—just awareness that official memory can't be trusted.

The collective instinct to save creates civic immunity.

A thousand archivists, acting separately, form a distributed conscience.

The Psychology of Distributed Trust

Gaslighting isolates.

Distributed memory reunites.

When you doubt your recollection but see your screenshot,

when others have the same file, the same quote—

the lie loses leverage.

The liar can still lie,

but the lie becomes visible rather than persuasive.

The receipts restore solidarity:

You're not crazy. You're not alone.

Historical Parallel · Samizdat

In the Soviet Union, *samizdat*—self-published manuscripts—circumvented state censorship.

Typed copies passed hand to hand.

The KGB destroyed presses, confiscated typewriters, arrested distributors.

It didn't matter.

Solzhenitsyn's *The Gulag Archipelago* circulated anyway.

Truth, multiplied by copies, escaped control.

Today, the network performs the same function at planetary scale.

Delete one copy—thousands remain.

The Limits and Responsibilities

Distributed memory isn't flawless.

Volume: we can't save everything.

Verification: falsehoods get archived too.

Context: fragments need framing.

Weaponization: bad actors preserve truth selectively to harm others.

The answer isn't retreat—it's ethics.

- Verify before archiving.
- Preserve context.
- Archive without endorsing.
- Respect privacy.
- Note corrections when facts change.

Preserve truth, not just information.

Tools for the Shadow Press

Basic:

- Screenshot important claims.
- Save to multiple locations.
- Include source and date.

Intermediate:

- Use archive services.
- Download volatile content.
- Convert to static PDFs.

Advanced:

- Maintain your own archive.
- Contribute to collective ones.
- Verify before sharing.
- Teach others these skills.

Not paranoia—preparedness.

When institutions can rewrite, citizens must record.

The Shadow Press as Immune System

Distributed memory functions like an immune system.

Institutions—like organs—can be compromised.

When they produce toxins instead of truth,

redundant systems activate.

Independent journalists.

Citizen archivists.

Alternative platforms.

It's messy, imperfect, sometimes inflammatory—

but necessary for survival.

When institutional memory fails, distributed memory compensates.

When the Fog Meets the Lamp

When the fog accelerates, the question isn't *Who's right?*

It's *Who still has the file?*

The official narrative will always be cleaner, simpler, more confident.

But clarity lives in complexity.

A teenager researching Iraq finds official claims, later corrections, leaked doubts.

She asks her teacher: *"Why did everyone believe it?"*

Answer: because institutional archives favored one narrative.

Distributed archives preserved another.

Most saw the first.

Few looked for the second.

The work of clarity
is excavation.

Easy stories require no effort.

Truth requires digging.

Memory multiplied
becomes harder to gaslight.

The Soviet Union erased people from photos.

The West erases them from search results.

Both gaslight.

Both fail when enough people keep copies.

When a thousand people have the photo, airbrushing fails.

When a million archived the article before editing, revision becomes visible.

That's the power of distributed memory: not perfection, but resilience.

THE FAMILY ARCHIVE

The father closes the laptop.

The receipts remain.

Tomorrow, another story will shift.

Another phrase will drift.

Another memory will be contested.

But some will save it.

Archive it.

Remember it.

That's the resistance—one screenshot at a time.

Years from now, his daughter will teach her children:

"Before you believe it, verify it.

Before you share it, check it.

And always, always keep receipts."

The fog won't disappear.

But it will meet resistance—

not from one person,

but from millions—each keeping their own small archive.

That distributed memory—redundant, imperfect, persistent—

is how truth survives the age of editable reality.

Distributed memory isn't paranoia.
It's citizenship.

———

It's the folder named **Receipts.**

The screenshot album.

The downloaded video.

The printed article.

It's memory as resistance.

And resistance as remembrance.

Distributed memory resists gaslighting because gaslighting requires isolation—

your memory against their certainty.

But when ten people keep the same screenshot,

fifty remember the same quote,

a hundred save the same document—

DISTORTED

the fog thins.

Activists demand change.
Archivists prevent forgetting.

And together, they keep the lights on.

But even vigilance has limits—when everything becomes gaslight, the word itself starts to flicker.

That's where language itself begins to beg for rescue.

The Sound of Authority

While dissidents save receipts and archive screenshots, institutions engineer choreography

Institutions don't distort the way culture does.

They don't rely on rumor, feed loops, or viral outrage.

Their influence arrives through process—formal, careful, credentialed.

While dissidents save receipts, agencies prepare briefings.

Screenshots may capture the moment.

But memos shape the frame.

The most effective distortion isn't loud.

It speaks in measured tones, wears a flag pin, and cites the Congressional Budget Office.

"Structural headwinds."

"Revenue enhancements."

"Transitory inflation."

These terms aren't false.

They're simply softened—abstract ways of acknowledging risk while projecting control.

The facts are rarely the first thing you hear.
They're the final thing consensus will allow.

In _Presidential Decision Making: The Economic Policy Board_, Harvard professor and former White House advisor Roger B. Porter maps how economic policy moved through the Ford administration. His work isn't critique; it's an institutional diagram—who drafted recommendations, how disagreements were resolved, and how a unified message took shape.

Read in its own context, Porter's book is a clear record of executive procedure.

Read through the lens of _Distorted_, it reveals a pattern still operating now:

Raw information rarely emerges unchanged.

It passes through a system built to coordinate.

And coordination inevitably edits what the public receives.

Porter's case studies—the 1975 State of the Union tax proposals, the U.S.–U.S.S.R. grain negotiations, the 1976 footwear import decision—show the steps:

Departments submitted analyses from differing vantage points.

Committees debated assumptions, risks, and wording.

Recommendations were revised to reduce internal conflict.

Timing shifted to avoid unnecessary volatility.

Porter never argues these mechanisms existed to obscure truth.

But he does show they were designed to produce unity—a single position drawn from a complicated set of inputs.

Viewed through this lens, a structural pattern becomes visible: Language grew more measured as it moved upstream.

Urgency was moderated.

Edges were softened.

The final message reflected not only data, but the stability of the moment in which it was cleared for release.

None of this implies deception.

But it creates distance.

Distance between early drafts and final statements.

Distance between what departments argued and what the public heard.

Distance between policy complexity and presentation calm.

Modern economic briefings still echo this architecture.

Terms like "temporary softening," "phased implementation," or "revenue enhancements" follow the same impulse Porter documented —language accurate in content, tempered in tone.

Porter never pushes toward these contemporary parallels.

But the implications of his structure are unmistakable:

What reaches the microphone isn't only information.
It's information that has survived a process.
Information released at a moment the system considered stable enough to absorb.

This isn't cultural spin.

It's procedural filtering—an institutional instinct toward order.

A system built to coordinate will naturally choose language that reassures.

A system built to avoid internal conflict will smooth the roughest edges.

A system built to control complexity will distill the signal into something steadier.

Nothing in Porter's work signals malice.

But everything in his work shows structure.

A structural tendency to deliver careful statements.

A structural tendency to delay until alignment forms.

A structural tendency to flatten sharp turns before they appear in public.

And from that structure comes a recognizable pattern:

Not all distortion rises from culture.

Some of it descends from process—quiet, procedural, professional.

Some of it wears a suit.

27

COURAGE CULTURE
THE DISCIPLINE OF
ACTING ON WHAT YOU SEE

The red light above the microphone glows.

A host leans toward it—alone, calm, heartbeat steady.

Once she read from a teleprompter written by committees.

Now the words are hers.

The light means live.
It means risk.

It means no one can edit what comes next.

Her sponsors left months ago.

Her audience grew.

That was the trade: certainty for truth.

She takes a breath.

"Let's talk about what we're not supposed to."

That sentence is the quiet beginning of a **Courage Culture**—the instinct to speak before permission, to value honesty over applause.

The Architecture of Fear

Every era invents new ways to be silent.

Ours chose algorithms.

No need for censors when sponsorships vanish faster than context.

Say the wrong phrase and the inbox fills with rage, not reason.

The mob doesn't need coordination; it just needs momentum.

Corporations call it brand safety.

Universities call it inclusion.

Media calls it balance.

Each means the same thing: *Don't scare the advertisers.*

Fear became policy long before it became feeling.

And policy, once written, teaches reflex.

The Currency of Cowardice

Fear's economy runs on **Courage Credit**—social capital traded in silence.

Every withheld sentence earns safety points.

Spend them recklessly and you're exiled.

Earn enough and you're promoted to virtue.

> *This economy rewards tone*
> *over truth.*

Apology is its currency; outrage its interest rate.

But the market is collapsing—too many apologies chasing too little trust.

Portraits of Courage

These portraits draw from recent, well-documented stories of public courage.

They're not fiction.

They're composites of people you've seen headline, trend, and vanish.

Portrait · The Broadcaster

A national host challenges a sacred script on live television.

Within hours, sponsors flee and colleagues go quiet.

Weeks later she reappears—smaller studio, freer voice, global audience.

The lesson spreads faster than her clips: independence is the new credibility.

Portrait · The Comedian

When jokes became regulated speech, one comic refused the memo.

Clubs canceled. Ticket sales doubled.

Laughter proved the crowd still wanted permission to think.

Portrait · The Novelist

A writer defended plain biology in public.

Publishers distanced; readers didn't.

Her stand turned fear into mirror—showing institutions what integrity looks like when it leaves the building.

Portrait · The Athlete

A competitor declined to chant the latest slogan.

Endorsements disappeared, but respect didn't.

In the highlight reel of history, performance fades; principle replays.

Portrait · The Professor

He questioned orthodoxy in an academic journal.

The article was retracted for "tone."

Colleagues uploaded it everywhere.

By suppressing it, the system made it immortal.

Portrait · The Artist

Her exhibition was pulled for "harmful imagery."

She rehung it herself.

The line outside stretched for blocks.

Courage always finds its audience.

―――

From Exiles to Examples

These people weren't trying to start a movement.

They were trying to keep their self-respect.

But exile creates clarity,
and clarity attracts company.

One voice becomes ten.

Ten becomes a culture.

By the end of 2024, that culture has a name.

They start calling it **Courage Culture**—not a brand, not an organization, but a signal.

An answer to cancellation that speaks softly and acts decisively.

The red lights are multiplying.

ASYMMETRICAL FEAR

In every era, certain ideas become immune to critique.

The proof isn't reverence; it's recoil.

Watch what happens when someone questions a doctrine that travels with its own blasphemy clause.

Even as you read this, you probably know one subject you're not supposed to mention.

The reflex isn't moral; it's survival.

That chill in the throat is the new censorship—self-installed.

In every era, some beliefs are safe to mock and others are treated as untouchable.

The difference rarely reflects holiness; it reflects who the culture fears.

Editors spike cartoons after threats.

Universities cancel speakers because security can't be guaranteed.

Activists who denounce Christian or Jewish symbols freely call caution "hate" when applied elsewhere.

The asymmetry speaks louder than the sermons.

Fear decides which blasphemies are allowed.

The silence isn't respect—it's calculation.

Editors pull cartoons.

Universities cancel speakers "for safety."

Journalists tiptoe around the same nouns they once printed freely.

Fear decides what counts as compassion.

In classrooms and newsrooms alike, you can feel the shift when people stop asking questions and start protecting feelings.

Once fear sets the syllabus, curiosity drops the class.

This is the blind spot of modern tolerance: it protects emotion but abandons proportion.

Real pluralism requires equal risk.

The Psychology of Courage

> *Courage isn't temperament; it's calibration —*
> *the decision to act while scared*
> *instead of silent while safe.*

Solomon Asch proved people will agree with a wrong answer to avoid isolation.

Stanley Milgram showed obedience can make decent people complicit.

Jonathan Haidt mapped how tribes defend feelings as moral facts.

Most conformity is unconscious; therefore most courage is teachable.

Fear spreads by mimicry.

So does steadiness.

One person asking *"Are we sure?"* can reset a room.

That moment is what this book calls **Moral Bandwidth**—the capacity to stay honest under pressure.

Every society has a limit.

When bandwidth collapses, distortion floods the line.

The Emerging Movement (Post 2024)

By late 2024, something shifted.

Independent media grew faster than legacy networks.

Artists banned for honesty became folk heroes.

Universities quietly reinstated debate as virtue.

The phrase **Courage Culture** began appearing in bios, intros, and classroom slides.

Not as organization—reflex.

A rebellion of steadiness.

Its language evolved in real time:

- **Courage Credit**—respect earned by risking truth with grace.
- **Re-entry Grace**—forgiving those who return after honest apology.
- **The Second Draft Principle**—revision over erasure; letting people grow.
- **#SpeakBeforePerfect**—the call to stop waiting for flawless words.
- **Moral Bandwidth**—a culture's tolerance for honesty.

Together they form the lexicon of recovery—the vocabulary of post-outrage sanity.

No movement is official until it names its virtues.

These names are catching.

The Blueprint

Courage Culture has rules of practice:

1. **Tell the truth calmly**—volume is vanity.
2. **Ask before agreeing**—the question is the antidote to conformity.
3. **Correct privately, question publicly**—dignity protects dialogue.
4. **Reward honesty early**—don't wait for crisis.
5. **Extend Re-entry Grace**—without forgiveness, courage becomes cruelty.
6. **Track Courage Credit**—remember who spoke when it cost something.

These aren't slogans; they're maintenance instructions for moral infrastructure.

The Counter-Contagion

Courage spreads faster than outrage once people see the exchange rate.

Outrage exhausts; courage restores.

Outrage isolates; courage recruits.

Outrage demands apology; courage offers re-entry.

Every public act of steadiness refuels private nerve.

Every apology accepted resets a system.

That's how cultural recovery begins—not with mobs switching sides, but with individuals refusing hysteria.

The Humor of Honesty

Satire is returning.

Comedians test the perimeter; audiences lean forward instead of reporting.

Laughter is the first sound a freed culture makes.

Humor proves proportion still lives.

A society that can laugh at itself is one step from healing.

THE BRIDGE · PRECISION OF COURAGE

Courage protects truth.

Language protects courage.

The next distortion arrives not through fear but through words—when *courage* itself gets redefined as *harm*, when disagreement becomes *violence.*

That's why the chapter ends here and the next begins.

Because after courage comes custody—of vocabulary, of meaning, of the lexicon we use to describe reality.

The red light is still glowing.

The microphones are multiplying.

And a culture learning to speak again is learning to live again.

> *Cancel Culture made fear contagious.*
> *Courage Culture is making honesty viral.*

The movement has begun.

Now we guard the language it breathes in.

28
WHEN ALL IS GASLIGHT
WHY PRECISION—NOT OUTRAGE —IS THE LAST ACT OF TRUST

A debate stage.

A politician interrupts: *"Stop gaslighting me!"*

The crowd roars.

The charge lands—not because it's accurate, but because the word itself has become a weapon.

Today, *gaslighting* shows up everywhere.

On TikTok, a bad breakup becomes *gaslighting*.

On Twitter, any disagreement is *gaslighting*.

By 2022, Merriam-Webster named it **Word of the Year.**

The word caught fire.

The meaning caught smoke.

But here's the risk:

When everything is gaslighting,
nothing is.

The Inflation of a Word

Gaslighting isn't just lying, spin, or one-off manipulation.

It's a sustained choreography:

- Deny what you saw.
- Reframe what you felt.
- Repeat until you doubt yourself.

That pattern is what makes it so corrosive.

When the word gets stretched to mean any argument or fib, it loses its edge.

And the people who suffer real gaslighting lose their word for it.

Psychologists used it clinically for decades before the public caught on.

Around 2016, it exploded into discourse.

By 2022, lookups rose 1,740 percent year-over-year.

People finally had a term for experiences they'd felt but couldn't name.

That mattered.

But popularity breeds dilution.

The Social-Media Effect

Online, *gaslighting* has become a catch-all insult:

- Someone disagrees? *Gaslighting.*
- A friend forgets your text? *Gaslighting.*
- A date cancels plans? *Gaslighting.*

Worse, it gives real gaslighters cover:

"Everyone says gaslighting these days. Don't be dramatic."

That dismissal is its own gaslight—real harm buried under word inflation.

The Word Isn't the Fog—Its Overuse Is

If the term becomes noise, the clarity it once gave is gone.

The same erosion swallowed words like *literally, trauma,* and *fake news.*

Stretch them too far, and they snap.

Gaslighting is too important to let it snap.

Politics and Performance

In politics, overuse is especially dangerous.

A candidate accused of corruption can smirk: *"You're gaslighting me."*

It works because the audience has heard it a thousand times.

Accuracy doesn't matter—the sting is in the soundbite.

Media and Meme Culture

Just as with *fake news,* ubiquity dulls force.

A phrase that once cracked open perception now risks parody.

Late-night hosts, TikTok trends, and meme accounts recycle it until weight turns to wink.

Popular memes—*"Gaslight, Gatekeep, Girlboss,"* or

"Tell me you're gaslighting without telling me you're gaslighting."—turn psychological abuse into punchline.

> *Humor isn't the enemy.*
> *Irony is the leak*
> *where meaning escapes.*

The Cascade of Lost Words

First, a word loses precision.

Then it loses restraint.

Finally, it loses meaning.

Fascist. Racist. Denier. Phobic.

Once grave accusations—now reflexive punctuation in public debate.

Each began as moral alarm and ended as rhetorical habit.

Every overreach dulls the signal until the word no longer warns—it performs.

When every offense is "extreme," real extremity disappears into the noise.

That's poetic truth at scale—emotion staged as evidence until outrage feels like fact.

> *Language doesn't collapse through censorship.*
> *It collapses through applause.*

Case Study · The Casual Label

A workplace dispute: one manager pushes a new system; another resists.

Someone mutters, *"Stop gaslighting me."*

Nothing fits the definition.

No denial of memory.

No erasure of perception.

Just conflict.

The danger isn't the misuse—it's the erosion.

When every conflict is called gaslighting, real survivors lose language.

The overuse becomes a second wound:

the same platforms that gave survivors words are now grinding them dull.

Identity and the Mirror

As seen earlier in this book, labels shape memory.

Survivors depend on precise words to anchor what happened.

If *gaslighting* blurs, the mirror they're fighting to trust fogs again.

Language is oxygen.

Without it, memory flickers.

Counter-Moves · Guarding the Word

- **Reserve it**—use *gaslighting* only for the choreography: deny → reframe → repeat.
- **Name other tactics precisely**—a lie is a lie; spin is spin; gaslighting is deeper.
- **Teach the difference**—clarity protects those who need the word most.

The word is powerful—if we keep it sharp.

Precision isn't pedantry.
It's survival.

Words are tools.

Overuse breaks them.

> *Language is a commons.*
> *Overuse depletes it.*
> *Precision preserves it.*

Gaslighting doesn't just steal reality.

Overuse steals the very word we need to fight it.

> *And when every signal feels corrupted,*
> *precision itself becomes the last act of trust.*

Because once words are repaired, sight follows.

29

TOWARD CLARITY

THE DISCIPLINE OF SEEING WITHOUT SPIN

The lights go out.

For a moment, the room is pitch black.

People shuffle—uncertain.

Then someone strikes a match.

A single flame glows, small but undeniable.

In its glow, the outlines of the room reappear.

Others light their matches.

*What was confusion
becomes clarity.*

That's gaslighting in reverse—

not floodlights, not instant revelation,

but steady flames: truths that cannot be talked out of existence.

The Journey So Far

We've walked through the gaslights of politics, media, education, culture, war, technology, medicine, and even our own homes.

Each arena twists perception differently,

but the choreography never changes—

deny the obvious, distort the felt, repeat until trust fractures.

The goal isn't persuasion.

It's dependence—training you to need the hand that blinds you.

Sidebar · When the Lie Feels Good

We don't just fall for distortions that oppose us.

We fall hardest for the ones that flatter us.

- Headlines that make "the other side" look foolish.
- Statistics that confirm our worldview.
- Stories too satisfying to double-check.

Gaslighting doesn't only exploit fear.

It exploits comfort.

The most dangerous lies
are the ones we want to be true.

Gaslighting doesn't always attack your beliefs.

Sometimes it hides inside them.

The Stakes of Forgetting

When societies stop resisting gaslighting,

history doesn't just repeat—it erases.

- Atrocities softened into "misunderstandings."
- Failures rewritten as victories.
- Lies footnoted into history.

The cost of surrendering truth isn't just confusion.

It's cultural amnesia.

> *A people that forgets*
> *doesn't choose its future.*
> *It inherits one.*

Naming the Flame

> *Once you see the pattern, you can name it.*
> *Once you name it, you can resist it.*

Throughout this book we've watched gaslighting wear disguises:

poetic truths posing as insight,

euphemisms as progress,

lies as ritual.

Naming the flame is saying:

"I know what I saw.

I know what I felt.

I refuse your fog."

The Discipline of Memory

Gaslighting collapses when memory holds.

> *Memory is not nostalgia —*
> *it's resistance.*

- Citizens archiving speeches.
- Families preserving untold stories.
- Communities recording contradictions.

Truth is fragile,

but memory makes it durable.

Paper outlives spin.

Diaries outlast slogans.

Memory is the only archive that regimes and corporations can't confiscate.

The Duty to Document

Truth unspoken is truth erased.

Every unkept record, every forgotten memory

becomes a lie the next generation must live under.

To resist, we document—

not for nostalgia, but for accountability.

Every receipt, every record, every testimony

is a safeguard against erasure.

The gaslighter thrives in silence.

> *To archive*
> *is to resist.*

The Role of Humor

Humor punctures fog faster than fury.

Laughing at absurd euphemisms—

"enhanced interrogation," "right-sizing," "mission accomplished"—

strips them of power.

The Role of Community

Gaslighting isolates; resistance reconnects.

No single flame clears the dark.
Together, they multiply.

- Families preserving stories.
- Journalists refusing euphemism.
- Teachers keeping inconvenient facts alive.

Community is the shield against distortion.

Where one person doubts, others confirm.

Shared truth is harder to erase.

Case Study · The Berlin Wall

When the Berlin Wall fell in 1989,

it wasn't toppled by tanks but by memory and persistence.

Citizens in the East were told life outside was bleak and failing.

Yet smuggled broadcasts, whispered stories, family letters said otherwise.

When the wall cracked, the rush west wasn't only political.

It was vindication of memory over propaganda—

a reminder that quiet truth outlasts loud control.

THE PRACTICE OF SLOW THINKING

Pause before reacting.

Breathe before believing.

Ask:

- Who benefits if I accept this version?
- What does the evidence say?
- What do I know, in my bones, to be true?

> *Clarity is rarely fast.*
> *But it is steady.*

THE COURAGE OF SMALL TRUTHS

Ultimate clarity isn't about solving everything.

It's about refusing to surrender small truths:

- *That did happen.*
- *That did hurt.*
- *That is what I saw.*

Small truths stacked together build a fortress.

> *Sanity isn't revelation.*
> *It's loyalty—*
> *to the truths we keep.*

And loyalty doesn't need a microphone.

It just needs to hold when the room goes quiet.

The Poetic Return

Poetic truth flatters our feelings;
real truth humbles them.

That's why clarity never comes cheap—it demands the courage to be uncomfortable.

Every generation must choose:

the story that soothes, or the evidence that stings.

The match you carry isn't metaphor.

It's discipline—the quiet, stubborn habit of seeing the world as it is,

even when the crowd applauds the illusion.

A Society of Matches

One flame reveals a room.

A million can remake a horizon.

Each person who resists—by archiving, by naming, by laughing, by remembering—adds flame to the collective.

Institutions can't extinguish them all.

The gaslight dims when enough people carry a flame—
because fog is fragile when it meets fire.

The Next Chapter is Yours

This book names the pattern.

You carry the light from here.

The real test begins after the last page—

at a dinner table, a ballot box, a boardroom,

or in a quiet moment of prayer.

Clarity is built by refusing to trade your memory

for someone else's story.

The question that remains:

Will you carry the match?

Clarity isn't permanent.

Like flame, it must be carried, renewed, and passed on—

or it flickers out.

This book ends here.

The practice doesn't.

The fog wants confusion.

The gaslight wants surrender.

But the flame—curiosity to clarity—

is yours to guard.

Guard it stubbornly.

Pass it generously.

The fog will return—

but so will the flame.

Strike one match, and the room is clear.

Strike millions, and night becomes day.

Truth isn't loud — it's loyal.
The flame doesn't shout; it stays.

EPILOGUE

LIVE LIT. EVEN WHEN THE WORLD BEGS YOU TO DIM.

Every generation inherits its own fog. Ours just happens to come wrapped in screens, hashtags, and algorithms. But in every age, someone strikes the first match. The story is not new. It is as old as power, as old as fear, as old as the human temptation to dim someone else's light in order to brighten your own.

This book has given you a framework, examples, and tools. But more than that, I hope it has given you something rarer: permission. Permission to trust your eyes. Permission to trust your gut. Permission to laugh at the absurd. Permission to walk through the world with your lamp unhidden.

Gaslighting works best when you feel alone—when you think you are the only one who noticed the timeline shift, the statistic bent, the headline that does not match the story. But you are not alone. Millions of others are rubbing their eyes, seeing the fog for what it is. And every time one person says, *"Wait, that doesn't add up,"* another lamp flickers on.

Here's the secret: clarity *is* contagious.

The work ahead does not begin with mobs. It begins with individuals —the teacher who preserves a story others want forgotten, the student who records a school board meeting before it is deleted, the neighbor who refuses to ignore what he saw, the worker who saves Slack screenshots when the announcement does not match the reality, the mother who teaches her child to notice when the words do not match the world. Gaslighting is designed to make you feel small, isolated, and powerless. But resistance does not begin with crowds. It begins with one person refusing to surrender their sight. One lamp lit in a room of darkness is enough to begin the chain.

———

History isn't written by whispers of safety.
It's written by those who stood when standing cost dearly.

Your lamp lights another, and soon the fog thins.

So what do you do now? You live lit. You choose reality over performance. Paper trail over rhetoric. Meaning over manipulation. Memory over fog. Not perfectly. Not always. But enough to keep the lamp alive.

The last gaslight is the lie that nothing can be done.
Do not believe it.

The fog feeds on silence. Lamps multiply on truth.
And if you've read this far, yours is one of them.

Live lit—especially when the world begs you to dim.
A single match—now eternal.

Coda: The Discipline of Clarity

Read slowly. Doubt confidently.
Question what feels obvious.

Keep what can be proven.

Remember: clarity isn't comfort.

Discomfort is the sound of thinking.

When the story flatters, test it.
When the headline glows, verify it.
When the crowd chants, count the voices.

Keep your own receipts.
Not for paranoia—for proportion.

The fog will always return.
But so will you.

One small light at a time.

Maxims of Distortion

Small truths that survive the fog

These are the distilled lines of *Distorted*—truths sharpened to their simplest form.

They are meant to be remembered, repeated, and carried into the fog when longer explanations fail.

———

I. Truth and Perception

The oldest trick in power isn't lying.
It's making you doubt you ever knew the truth.

Gaslighting doesn't erase memory.
It erodes confidence in it.

That's why gaslighting works—
it leans on what makes us human.

Reality doesn't vanish—it gets renamed.

The fog doesn't argue.
It hums.

Truth is not fragile.
It's simply quieter than the lie.

Memory is not nostalgia.
It is resistance.

Paper outlives spin.
Diaries outlast slogans.

Silence is not neutrality.
It's the sound of editing in progress.

The first story always feels true.
That's why correction sounds like betrayal.

II. POETIC TRUTH

Poetic truth doesn't erase facts.
It outshines them.

Poetic truth flatters feeling.
Real truth humbles it.

Every age wraps its lies in virtue
and calls it progress.

The story that soothes
will always outsell the evidence that stings.

Clarity never comes cheap.
It demands the courage to be uncomfortable.

The match you carry isn't metaphor—
it's discipline.

A story that explains reality can serve it.
A story that replaces reality rules it.

Gaslighting makes you doubt what you saw.
Poetic truth makes you love what never was.

III. Language and Power

Euphemism doesn't hide harm.
It teaches you to rename it.

Every euphemism is a mask
that fits the mouth of power.

Control the dictionary,
and you control the debate.

Words shape permission
before they shape belief.

Language stops revealing
the moment it starts reassuring.

Precision isn't cruelty.
It's respect.

IV. Institutions and Authority

Power doesn't need truth.
It needs compliance.

Institutions don't need belief.
They need obedience.

Procedure isn't truth;
it's theater performed for doubt.

Whoever controls the curriculum
controls the future.

When protection replaces preparation,
education becomes indoctrination.

The robe can be costume,
the gavel a prop,
the transcript a script.

Once law loses its moral anchor,
legality becomes performance.

Justice unrecorded
is justice rewritten.

Archive proof.

The ceremony of accountability
often replaces accountability itself.

V. Media and Technology

The lie gets the billboard.
The truth gets the broom.

The lie trends.
The correction hides.

Free platforms sell something,
usually you.

Screens don't show reality.
They curate it.

The algorithm doesn't lie.
It decides what you're allowed to see.

Transparency without accountability
is still manipulation.

Every feed is a hall of mirrors.
The only question is who built the glass.

Speed rewards error faster than truth can wake up.
The louder the headline, the quieter the correction.

VI. Culture and Memory

History isn't what happened.
It's what institutions decide we'll remember.

Culture gaslights not by telling you you're wrong—
but by telling you you're alone.

Dismissal is its own gaslight.

A people who forget
don't choose their future.
They inherit one.

The greener the ad,
the dirtier the ledger.

The trophy shines.
The scars stay hidden.

In war, the first casualty isn't truth.
It's memory.

Redundant memory is freedom's insurance.

VII. Identity and The Self

Identity gaslighting doesn't just distort facts.
It distorts the mirror.

The strongest act of resistance
is trusting your own reflection.

Labels offer shorthand—
until they become cages.

Every label is a mirror.
Clarity begins when you decide where to look.

The self you perform can eclipse the self you are.

VIII. Human Nature

Fear makes obedience feel like reason.

Exhaustion is the gaslighter's favorite tool.

We remember emotion longer than evidence.

The hardest person to deprogram
is the one who thinks they never were.

Clarity begins
when curiosity outweighs comfort.

Humor punctures fog
faster than fury.

Small truths stacked together
build a fortress.

Receipts are rebellion.

Clarity isn't permanent.
It's practiced.

Confusion is not chaos;
it's control disguised as noise.

IX. ADVERSITY

Adversity is not the fog.
It's the match.

Shield someone from adversity,
and you steal their strength.

Without difficulty,
clarity atrophies.

Comfort is a story;
growth is a practice.

Avoid discomfort long enough,
and confusion feels like safety.

X. FUTURE AND RESISTANCE

Prediction dressed as destiny
is manipulation in future tense.

The future is the only place
where lies can live tax-free.

You can't archive
what you're afraid to name.

The question that remains is simple:
Will you carry the match?

Clarity is a practice,
not a destination.

One small light at a time.

When the future is sold as certain,
someone already wrote the script.

ENDNOTES
NOTES, SOURCES, AND WORKS CONSULTED

THE RECORD AND THE FOG

Every fact in this book began somewhere else—in a study, a headline, a footnote, a confession.

What follows isn't exhaustive; it's representative.

These are the sources that anchored the work when memory blurred and narrative pressed too hard.

They remain the receipts—the record against the fog.

————

Chapter 1 · The Original Trick
Patrick Hamilton, *Gas Light* (1938 play); George Cukor, *Gaslight* (1944).
Elizabeth F. Loftus & John C. Palmer, "Reconstruction of Automobile Destruction," *Journal of Verbal Learning and Verbal Behavior* (1974).
Daniel Kahneman, *Thinking, Fast and Slow* (2011).
Kate Abramson, "Turning Up the Lights on Gaslighting," *Philosophical Perspectives* 28 (2014).

Chapter 2 · Doubt, by Design
Leon Festinger, *A Theory of Cognitive Dissonance* (1957).
Solomon E. Asch, "Opinions and Social Pressure," *Scientific American* (1955).
Stanley Milgram, *Obedience to Authority* (1974).
Daniel Kahneman & Amos Tversky, "Judgment under Uncertainty," *Science* (1974).

Chapter 3 · Poetic Truth
Jonathan Haidt, *The Righteous Mind* (2012).
Yuval Noah Harari, *Sapiens* (2014).
Robert B. Cialdini, *Influence* (rev. ed. 2021).
Malcolm Gladwell, *Blink* (2005).

Chapter 4 · The Money Script
Edward Bernays, *Propaganda* (1928).
Shoshana Zuboff, *The Age of Surveillance Capitalism* (2019).
Financial Crisis Inquiry Commission, *The Financial Crisis Inquiry Report* (2011).
Michael Lewis, *The Big Short* (2010).

Chapter 5 · The Memory Hack
Daniel L. Schacter, *The Seven Sins of Memory* (2001).
Aleida Assmann, *Cultural Memory and Western Civilization* (2011).
Pew Research Center, "Americans' Trust in Media and Institutions" (latest).
Larry Sanger interviews, "Wikipedia and the Politics of Knowledge," 2023–2024.

Chapter 6 · The Media Mirror
Neil Postman, *Amusing Ourselves to Death* (1985).
Marshall McLuhan, *Understanding Media* (1964).
Claire Wardle & Hossein Derakhshan, *Information Disorder, Council of Europe Report* (2017).
Gallup/Knight Foundation, "American Views: Trust, Media, and Democracy" (2022).
Claire Wardle, *Understanding Information Disorder*, Harvard Shorenstein Center (2019).

Chapter 7 · The War on Words
George Orwell, *Politics and the English Language* (1946).
William Lutz, *Doublespeak* (1989).
Steven Pinker, *The Stuff of Thought* (2007).
Deborah Cameron, *Verbal Hygiene* (1995).
Merriam-Webster editorial archives, "Definition Updates 2020–2023."

Chapter 8 · The Political Frame
Walter Lippmann, *Public Opinion* (1922).
Hannah Arendt, *The Origins of Totalitarianism* (1951).
Pew Research Center, "Public Trust in Government: 1958–2024."
Merriam-Webster, "Word of the Year: Gaslighting" (2022).

Chapter 9 · The Cultural Rewrite
Douglas Murray, *The Madness of Crowds* (2019).
Greg Lukianoff & Jonathan Haidt, *The Coddling of the American Mind* (2018).
Camille Paglia, *Sexual Personae* (1990).
René Girard, *Violence and the Sacred* (1972).
Pew Research Center, "Cultural Polarization and Media Consumption" (2023).

Chapter 10 · The Classroom Rewrite
Diane Ravitch, *The Death and Life of the Great American School System* (2010).
Allan Bloom, *The Closing of the American Mind* (1987).
NAEP (U.S. Dept. of Education), *Nation's Report Card* (latest).
Jonathan Haidt, *The Anxious Generation* (2024).

Chapter 11 · Procedure as Performance
Michelle Alexander, *The New Jim Crow* (2010).
U.S. Sentencing Commission, "Overview of Federal Criminal Cases."
Bryan Stevenson, *Just Mercy* (2014).
Alexander Hamilton, *Federalist No. 78.*

Chapter 12 · The Vanished Agreement
Amy C. Edmondson, *The Fearless Organization* (2018).

Gallup, *State of the Global Workplace* (2023).
Bethany McLean & Peter Elkind, *The Smartest Guys in the Room* (2003).

Chapter 13 · When Care Distorts
Atul Gawande, *Being Mortal* (2014).
Abigail Shrier, *Bad Therapy* (2024).
CDC COVID-19 mortality dashboards (2020–2022).
Barry Meier, *Pain Killer* (2003).

Chapter 14 · The Tech Trap
Tristan Harris et al., *The Social Dilemma* (Netflix, 2020).
Shoshana Zuboff, *The Age of Surveillance Capitalism* (2019).
Safiya Umoja Noble, *Algorithms of Oppression* (2018).
Cal Newport, *Digital Minimalism* (2019).
Chamath Palihapitiya, remarks at Stanford GSB (2017).

Chapter 15 · The Insurance Illusion
California Dept. of Insurance, "Wildfire Risk and Non-Renewals" (2023).
National Association of Insurance Commissioners, *Market Trend Reports* (latest).
KFF, *Employer Health Benefits Survey* (2023).

Chapter 16 · The Spectacle
PBS Frontline, *League of Denial* (2013).
Taylor Branch, "The Shame of College Sports," *The Atlantic* (2011).
U.S. Senate Judiciary Committee, "Testimony of Gymnastics Survivors" (2021).
Ben Fritz, *The Big Picture* (2018).

Chapter 17 · The Gospel of Power
Alister E. McGrath, *Christian Theology: An Introduction* (2017).
U.S. House Jonestown Hearings (1979).
Peter L. Berger, *The Sacred Canopy* (1967).
Pew Research Center, "Faith in America: Belief and Belonging" (2023).

Chapter 18 · The Fringe Effect
Jacques Vallée, *Revelations* (1991).
Raymond A. Moody, *Life After Life* (1975).
Fiona Broome, *MandelaEffect.com* (archive).
Graham Hancock, *Magicians of the Gods* (2015).
Leslie Kean, *UFOs: Generals, Pilots, and Government Officials Go on the Record* (2010).

Chapter 19 · The Distorted Reflection
Erving Goffman, *The Presentation of Self in Everyday Life* (1959).
Jean M. Twenge, *iGen* (2017).
Abigail Shrier, *Irreversible Damage* (2020).
Charles Taylor, *The Ethics of Authenticity* (1992).

Chapter 20 · The Artificial Gaslight
Gary Marcus, "AI Hype vs. AI Reality," *New Yorker* (2023).

Robert Chesney & Danielle Citron, "Deep Fakes and the New Disinformation," *California Law Review* 107 (2019).
C. Thi Nguyen, "Echo Chambers and Epistemic Bubbles," *Episteme* (2020).
Timnit Gebru et al., "On the Dangers of Stochastic Parrots," *FAccT Proceedings* (2021).
Emily M. Bender et al., "On the Dangers of Stochastic Parrots: Can Language Models Be Too Big?" *FAccT Proceedings* (2021).

Chapter 21 · Tomorrow, Sold Today
Alvin Toffler, *Future Shock* (1970).
IPCC, *Global Warming of 1.5 °C* (2018).
Frank Furedi, *How Fear Works* (2018).
Peter Zeihan, *The End of the World Is Just the Beginning* (2022).

Chapter 22 · The Masculine Mirage
Jean M. Twenge, *Generations* (2023).
Richard Reeves, *Of Boys and Men* (2022).
National Center for Education Statistics (NCES), "Undergraduate Enrollment by Sex, 1970–2023."
Centers for Disease Control and Prevention (CDC), "Suicide Mortality in the United States."
Pew Research Center, "Online Dating and Women's Experiences on Dating Apps" (2023).
Pew Research Center, "Political Polarization and Ideological Shifts Among Young Adults" (2023).
Gillette, "We Believe: The Best Men Can Be" campaign film (2019).
Jonathan Haidt, *The Anxious Generation* (2024).
Jordan B. Peterson, *12 Rules for Life* (2018).
Joe Rogan Experience archives, interviews on cultural shifts and masculinity, 2018–2024.
Greg Lukianoff & Jonathan Haidt, *The Coddling of the American Mind* (2018).
Pew Research Center, "Global Populist Support Trends Among Young Men" (2023).
German Federal Election Studies (GLES), youth support trends for AfD (2023).
Argentine National Electoral Data, youth vote share for Javier Milei (2023).
Abigail Shrier, *Bad Therapy* (2024).
Tim Urban, *What's Our Problem?* (2023).
Marshall McLuhan, *Understanding Media* (1964).
Claire Wardle, "Information Disorder" (Harvard Shorenstein Center, 2019).

Chapter 23 · The Family Lens
Jean Piaget, *The Child's Conception of the World* (1929).
Erich Fromm, *The Art of Loving* (1956).
Abigail Shrier, *Bad Therapy* (2024).
Pew Research Center, "Parenting in America" (2023).

Chapter 24 · The Small Distortions
Robin Stern, *The Gaslight Effect* (2007).
Erving Goffman, *Frame Analysis* (1974).
Robert B. Cialdini, *Influence* (rev. ed. 2021).

Chapter 25 · Resisting the Gaslight
Viktor E. Frankl, *Man's Search for Meaning* (1946).
Daniel Kahneman, Olivier Sibony & Cass Sunstein, *Noise* (2021).
Jonathan Haidt, *The Happiness Hypothesis* (2006).
Judith Herman, *Trauma and Recovery* (1992).

Chapter 26 · The Shadow Press
Daniel Ellsberg, *Secrets* (2002).
Jean Heller, "Syphilis Victims in U.S. Study Went Untreated," *Associated Press* (July 26, 1972).
Marshall McLuhan & Quentin Fiore, *The Medium is the Massage* (1967).
Brewster Kahle, *Internet Archive Mission Statement* (archive.org).
Martin Gurri, *The Revolt of the Public* (2018).

Intermezzo · The Sound of Authority
Roger B. Porter, *Presidential Decision Making: The Economic Policy Board* (Cambridge University Press, 1980). Porter's analysis of the Ford administration's Economic Policy Board includes case studies of the 1975 State of the Union tax proposals, the U.S.–U.S.S.R. grain negotiations, and the 1976 footwear import decision. The interpretive framing in this intermezzo reflects the author's analysis of the structural implications of Porter's process descriptions.

Chapter 27 · Courage Culture
Jonathan Haidt, *The Anxious Generation* (2024).
Douglas Murray, *The War on the West* (2022).
Abigail Shrier, *Bad Therapy* (2024).
Tim Urban, *What's Our Problem?* (2023).

Chapter 28 · When All Is Gaslight
Deborah Tannen, *The Argument Culture* (1998).
Steven Pinker, *The Stuff of Thought* (2007).
Merriam-Webster, "Word of the Year: Gaslighting" (2022).
Jonathan Rauch, *The Constitution of Knowledge* (2021).

Chapter 29 · Toward Clarity
George Orwell, *1984* (1949).
Aleksandr Solzhenitsyn, *The Gulag Archipelago* (1973).
Jonathan Rauch, *The Constitution of Knowledge* (2021).
Michael Polanyi, *Personal Knowledge* (1958).

The Clarity Toolkit · Framework and Practice
Greg Lukianoff & Jonathan Haidt, *The Coddling of the American Mind* (2018).
Douglas Murray, *The War on the West* (2022).
Abigail Shrier, *Bad Therapy* (2024).
Tim Urban, *What's Our Problem?* (2023).
Jonathan Haidt et al., *The Anxious Generation* (2024).

Suggested Reading · The Clarity and Resilience Shelf

Jonathan Haidt & Greg Lukianoff, *The Canceling of the American Mind* (2023).
Sebastian Junger, *Tribe* (2016).
Roger Scruton, *How to Be a Conservative* (2014).
Abigail Shrier, *Bad Therapy* (2024).
Thomas Sowell, *A Conflict of Visions* (2007).
Tim Urban, *What's Our Problem?* (2023).

END OF DISTORTED

(Because every age needs its receipts.)

THE GLOSSARY OF FOG
A FIELD GUIDE TO DISTORTION

"Every age invents its own vocabulary for denial. Because language is the first battlefield."

— Jim Detjen

———

This isn't a dictionary. It's a decoder ring.

These are the words, phrases, and slogans that blur reality by sounding good while meaning less.

Each entry strips away euphemism to expose what hides beneath the fog.

A

Accountability Theater — Performative outrage or "internal review" designed to restore confidence, not truth. *The spotlight replaces the cleanup.*
See also: transparency theater, institutional gaslighting

AI Hallucination — A machine's confident fabrication, fluent but false. *Fluency masquerading as fact.*
See also: synthetic transparency, automation bias, media mirror

Algorithmic Colonialism — The export of one culture's values through another's data. *Empire never ended—it updated its code.*
See also: information fog, automation bias

Algorithmic Curation — The invisible hand deciding what you see, disguised as "your feed." *Personalization is preselection.*
See also: filter bubble, synthetic transparency

Alternative Facts — Lies dressed for a press conference.
See also: spin, poetic truth

Authenticity Marketing — The corporate art of selling sincerity. *Even the apology is A/B-tested.*
See also: brand virtue, moral licensing

B

Beyond Petroleum — A corporate rebrand that made oil sound like virtue. *Logo in bloom, pipeline in shadow.*
See also: greenwashing, stakeholder capitalism

Brand Humanization — When corporations speak like friends. *"We're listening," says the logo.*
See also: authenticity marketing

Brand Virtue — Moral storytelling for sale. *Conscience as commodity.*
See also: greenwashing, moral licensing

Broken Window Effect — The normalization of small lies until whole systems warp. *Decay becomes décor.*
See also: everyday gaslighting, truth decay

C

Carbon Footprint — A metric invented to transfer guilt from corporations to consumers. *Count your straws, not our spills.*
See also: greenwashing, moral licensing

Carbon Neutral — Mathematically correct, morally incomplete.
Balance sheet serenity, planetary noise.
See also: net zero, stakeholder capitalism

Collateral Damage — Bureaucratic shorthand for civilian death.
See also: fog of war, euphemism drift

Confirmation Bias — The comfort of believing what flatters us.
The mirror we never clean.
See also: poetic truth, truth decay

Conscious Collection — A fast-fashion fig leaf; guilt-free consumption at 1% of the catalog.
See also: greenwashing

Crisis Monetization — Turning catastrophe into profit. *Every emergency has a sponsor.*
See also: hope marketing

D

Data Dignity — The idea that your information is labor—and should be paid as such. *Your clicks are work unpaid.*
See also: surveillance capitalism

Deflection Strategy — "What about them?" as policy.
See also: whataboutism

Denial Loop — The choreography of distortion: deny, reframe, repeat.

See also: institutional gaslighting, poetic truth

Digital Amnesia — Forgetting faster because everything's saved. *Memory outsourced to the cloud—and lost there.*
See also: information fatigue

Disinformation Laundering — The repetition of lies until they read as truth. *Echo long enough, and the sound becomes evidence.*
See also: truth decay, spin

Downsizing — Layoffs reframed as efficiency.
See also: corporate gaslighting

E

Emotional Truth — A feeling that substitutes for evidence. *The heart takes the stand; facts plead the Fifth.*
See also: poetic truth, confirmation bias

Enhanced Interrogation — Torture with a thesaurus.
See also: collateral damage

Euphemism Drift — When words age into anesthesia. *The softer the term, the sharper the harm.*
See also: spin, linguistic capture

F

Fact-Checker's Paradox — The more we outsource truth, the less we trust it.
See also: referee problem, synthetic transparency

Fact-Checking Fatigue — The exhaustion that comes from endless corrections. *The truth arrives tired.*
See also: misinformation theater

Fake News — A once-useful term blunted into noise; now a synonym for "anything I dislike."
See also: truth decay

Filter Bubble — Your worldview, algorithmically shrink-wrapped.
See also: algorithmic curation

Fog of War — When violence is renamed "strategy."
See also: collateral damage

G

Gaslighting — The systematic erosion of trust in one's perception: deny, reframe, repeat.
See also: institutional gaslighting, poetic truth

Green Hushing — The new corporate modesty: under-promising progress to avoid scrutiny. *Silence, sold as humility.*
See also: greenwashing

Greenwashing — The art of marketing virtue while manufacturing harm. *The greener the ad, the dirtier the ledger.*
See also: brand virtue, moral licensing, carbon footprint

H

Historical Revisionism — When textbooks trade truth for favor.
See also: institutional gaslighting

Hope Marketing — Selling redemption instead of reform.
See also: crisis monetization

Humanitarian Washing — Empathy as camouflage. *Care is cheaper than change.*

I

Influencer Diplomacy — Governments hiring creators to sell policy. *Foreign affairs by selfie.*
See also: media mirror

Information Fog — Data density so thick it hides direction. *The flood conceals the drought.*
See also: algorithmic colonialism, digital amnesia

Information Fatigue — Knowing so much you stop noticing.
See also: digital amnesia

Institutional Gaslighting — When systems tell you the policy is fine—you're the problem.
See also: accountability theater, transparency theater

J–L

Just Following Orders — Bureaucratic absolution for moral surrender.
See also: institutional gaslighting

Linguistic Capture — Winning the argument by rewriting the dictionary mid-debate.
See also: spin, euphemism drift

Luxury Minimalism — Owning less, expensively.
See also: moral licensing

M

Media Mirror — The illusion that reflection equals truth. *You see what sees you back.*

See also: synthetic transparency, ai hallucination

Metacrisis — The framing that everything connects, used to justify control.
See also: hope marketing

Misinformation Theater — The staged cleanup of chaos.
Moderation for the cameras.
See also: fact-checking fatigue, synthetic transparency

Mission Accomplished — Premature triumph as strategy.
See also: poetic truth

Moral Fatigue — When compassion burns out before change begins.
See also: moral licensing

Moral Licensing — One good deed as permission for the next harm.
See also: greenwashing, brand virtue

Mostly Peaceful — The caption that contradicts the picture.
See also: poetic truth

N–P

Net Zero — The accounting trick that lets harm cancel itself.
See also: carbon neutral

News Desert — A community where journalism has died and rumor has moved in.
See also: truth decay

Operational Pause — A delay renamed as discipline.
See also: bureaucratic spin

Performance of Accountability — The public ritual of pretending to care.
See also: accountability theater

Poetic Truth — The story that feels right but falsifies reality. *The lyric that replaces the ledger.*
See also: emotional truth, confirmation bias, mission accomplished

Progress Narrative — The myth that "new" means "better." *Innovation as ideology.*
See also: metacrisis

Q–S

Quiet Quitting — Boundaries reframed as betrayal.
See also: resilience culture

Reputation Laundering — Philanthropy as absolution.
See also: stakeholder capitalism

Resilience Culture — When exhaustion is glamorized as grit. *The machine praises your endurance so it never has to rest.*
See also: quiet quitting, wellness industrial complex

Shadow Banning — Visibility theft disguised as neutrality.
See also: synthetic transparency

Spin — The ancestor of modern gaslights. *The wheel that never stops turning.*
See also: linguistic capture, poetic truth

Stakeholder Capitalism — Ethics outsourced to marketing.
See also: greenwashing

Synthetic Transparency — Openness curated for optics.
See also: transparency theater, media mirror

Transparency Theater — When "open data" hides the important parts.
See also: synthetic transparency, accountability theater

Truth Decay — The slow corrosion of shared reality. *Facts die quietly, under applause.*
See also: confirmation bias, poetic truth

Weaponized Empathy — Using compassion to disarm critique. *"If you cared, you'd agree."*
See also: humanitarian washing

Wellness Industrial Complex — Selling calm while fueling exhaustion. *Breathe in. Buy more.*
See also: resilience culture

You're Overreacting — The gaslighter's first line of defense—and sometimes their last.
See also: gaslighting

The fog doesn't erase words.
It just teaches them to lie more politely.

Unwritten Chapters
This book isn't afraid of difficult topics—only distorted ones

Some subjects today are so charged, so linguistically booby-trapped, that writing about them almost guarantees distortion before the first paragraph is read.

The purpose of *Distorted* isn't to settle those debates. It's to give you a framework for seeing how they're fought.

I touch several of these subjects in passing—not to score points, but to expose the method beneath the message.

Still, there are others I've chosen not to address directly—not because they aren't relevant, but because they've become so emotionally radioactive that nuance rarely survives contact.

What follows isn't a catalog of avoidance. It's an open invitation.

Use the same framework—gaslighting, poetic truth, framing, and moral inversion—to test how these conversations are being shaped in real time.

Politics, Law & Government

Power, policy, enforcement, and narrative control.

- **January 6 and political violence**—definitions, accountability, and the "insurrection" narrative.
- **Election integrity & "defending democracy."**
- **Administrative power**—agency deference and the myth of expertise.
- **Affirmative action after SFFA.**
- **Censorship framed as "safety."**
- **Domestic terrorism & white-nationalism narratives.**
- **Public-health authority**—mandates, masking, memory.
- **War coverage**—precision language vs. civilian reality.
- **Free speech vs. "harmful speech."**
- **Religion in public life.**
- **Patriotism, shame, and the modern nation.**
- **Consent and coercion**—the shifting definitions of harm, agency, and memory.
- **The jobless utopia**—automation, identity, and the economics of erasure.
- **Campus adjudication and due process**—when safety narratives override evidence and rights collapse by design.

⊕ Media, Tech & Algorithms

Information environments, narrative engineering, and distortion delivery systems.

- **AI ethics & governance**—bias, censorship, and techno-moral panic.
- **Foreign-owned apps & algorithmic influence.**
- **Net neutrality & digital gatekeepers.**
- **UAPs and government whistleblowers**—secrecy, disclosure theater, and the psychology of disbelief.
- **ESG and corporate virtue.**
- **Student-loan relief**—major questions vs. moral storytelling.
- **The biometric bargain**—surveillance, consent, and the myth of safety.
- **Childhood under code**—algorithmic identity formation and digital parenting.

How people perform identity, seek belonging, and wrestle with narrative control.

- **The history of LGB (pre-TQI+)**—what changed, when, and why the acronyms now carry politics.
- **Men competing in women's sports**—fairness, safety, and linguistic policing.
- **Title IX reinterpretations**—sex vs. gender identity; shifting grievance standards.
- **Ideology in universities**—gatekeeping, DEI mandates, compelled speech.
- **Antifa activism and the language of antifascism**—moral branding, media framing, and permissible chaos.
- **Ideological violence and selective silence**—from Antifa to gender-activist extremism, and how coverage bends by cause.
- **Mental-health culture and "trauma-language."**—where therapy meets ideology.
- **Resilience vs. fragility**—the generational psychology of safetyism.
- **Social contagion in identity**—narratives of affirmation and moral inflation.
- **Parenting, overdiagnosis, and moral outsourcing.**
- **Disability and moral optics**—performance, invisibility, and the weaponization of inspiration.
- **Neurodivergence narratives**—diagnosis, identity, and the blur between advocacy and overreach.
- **Racial essentialism and the new orthodoxy**—identity, guilt, and the flattening of history.
- **Allyship as optics**—performance, guilt, and the outsourcing of virtue.

🧾 Institutions & Bureaucratic Framing

Where euphemism replaces evidence—and spin becomes structure.

- **Climate policy & energy mandates.**
- **Policing, bail, and crime data.**
- **Guns, rights, and risk.**
- **Immigration enforcement vs. humanitarian framing.**
- **Abortion after Dobbs**—state vs. national policy; "rights" vs. "protections."
- **IVF and embryo personhood**—liability, access, and moral language.
- **Chemical comfort**—pharma narratives, diagnostic inflation, and the cost of trust.
- **Food, shame, and the purity myth**—when wellness becomes orthodoxy.
- **Monetized selfhood**—hustle culture, gig work, and the collapse of meaning into metrics.

🎭 Culture, Symbols & Moral Language

THE THEATRE OF VIRTUE, SHAME, AND MORAL PERFORMANCE.

- **BLM and policing narratives**—protest vs. riot, reform vs. rhetoric.
- **Israel / Palestine and Middle-East framing**—AIPAC influence, moral equivalence, civilian casualties, selective empathy.
- **The Masculine Mirage**—indirectly referenced, culturally central.
- **ANTIFA**—listed separately, symbolically potent across factions.
- **The Professionalization of Silence**—career survival through moral fog.
- **The MeToo pendulum**—from truth-telling to trial-by-narrative, and the collapse of nuance between justice and mob.

———

These aren't off-limits topics.

They're ongoing experiments in distortion.

Don't wait for permission to question them.

Apply the lens. Test the frame.

The truth doesn't fear inquiry—only control does.

Afterword

I did not set out to write about politics, media, culture, or technology. I set out to write about trust—how fragile it is, how powerful it is, and how easily it can be stolen.

Along the way, I realized something: gaslighting is not just "out there" in headlines or history books. It happens in kitchens, classrooms, workplaces—even in our own thoughts. Every one of us has, at some point, felt that flicker of doubt: *Am I the crazy one? Did I imagine it? Am I the only one who sees this?*

You are not.

This book is my attempt to hand you three things: a language, a framework, and a lantern. Language to name what is happening. A framework to see the pattern. And a lantern to carry into the fog— because you never fight darkness with words alone. You fight it with light.

I do not expect you to agree with every example, or to read every chapter as gospel. That is not the point. The point is to notice. To pause. To trust your instincts again. Because if enough people do that —if enough lamps stay lit—the fog does not stand a chance.

Thank you for trusting me with your time, your attention, and your willingness to wrestle with hard questions. That, in itself, is an act of clarity.

Stay lit.
Stay questioning.
Stay free.

This book is for anyone who ever doubted their own eyes—and chose to trust them anyway.

Acknowledgments

This book was not written in isolation.

To my family—thank you for being my first mirrors, the ones who reflected truth back when the fog pressed in.

To my wife, Reina—your steadiness and light kept mine burning.

To my children—your courage, curiosity, and clarity inspire every page.

To my mentors and teachers—thank you for showing me that clarity is both a craft and a discipline.

To the thinkers, friends, and colleagues who pushed me to sharpen arguments and test examples—your questions kept the lamps burning.

To my readers, listeners, and supporters—thank you for trusting me with your attention. In an age where distraction rules, that trust is no small gift.

And finally, to those who resist gaslighting in their own lives, often quietly and without recognition—

this book is for you.

About the Author

Jim Detjen is the founder of **Gaslight 360** and host of the podcast *Think First*. Through his writing, teaching, and media work, he equips readers and listeners to recognize manipulation, resist narrative spin, and reclaim perspective. His work examines how stories influence power, perception, and decision-making—and how clarity can be restored when narrative replaces evidence.

Jim began his career in the U.S. Army's **3rd Infantry Regiment—The Old Guard**, the Army's oldest active-duty infantry unit and its most elite ceremonial command. Tasked with honoring fallen heroes, guarding the Tomb of the Unknown Soldier, and representing the nation in its most symbolic moments, The Old Guard operates where error is not an option. There, he served in an environment shaped by discipline, preparation, and trust—values that continue to influence how he leads, listens, and thinks.

For more than twenty-five years, Jim has advised global brands, academic institutions, and nonprofit boards at the intersection of brand architecture, strategic partnerships, and sustainable growth. Whether working publicly or behind the scenes, he focuses on connecting story, structure, and scale—and aligning them with reality.

His work spans fields where influence is shaped and narratives are formed—from athletics and music to technology and public life. The work he values most, however, happens quietly: mentoring talent, building community, and passing on principles that do not trend, but endure.

At home, Jim is most proud of his role as husband and father. His family's path reflects a shared commitment to excellence and curiosity, including children pursuing advanced studies at **Harvard** and the **United States Air Force Academy**.

———

For more books, the podcast, and updates:
www.JimDetjen.com